FIRE IN THE MACHINE

DRIVING ENTREPRENEURIAL
INNOVATION
IN LARGE CPG ORGANIZATIONS

JONATHAN TOFEL & CAROLINA SASSON

FIRE IN THE MACHINE
Driving Entrepreneurial Innovation in Large CPG Organizations

ISBN 978-1-5445-3017-8 *Hardcover*

978-1-5445-3016-1 *Paperback*

978-1-5445-3015-4 *Ebook*

978-1-5445-3018-5 *Audiobook*

CONTENTS

INTRODUCTION

"The consumer packaged goods industry grew 10.3 percent last year and small suppliers and private label manufacturers accounted for 51 percent of total growth... Small manufacturers gained an additional 1.1 percent [of total share]. Large manufacturers...saw their share reduced for the fifth consecutive year."

—GEORGE ANDERSON, RetailWire[1]

It doesn't seem possible that a startup composed of three people and a dream could challenge a multibillion-dollar Fortune 500 company with seemingly inexhaustible resources, yet it's happening every day in the world of consumer packaged goods (CPG).

1 George Anderson, "Are Small Brands Eating Big Food's Lunch?" RetailWire, January 29, 2021, https://retailwire.com/discussion/are-small-brands-eating-big-foods-lunch/.

But this isn't a book about championing startups and declaring that David has beat Goliath. Quite the opposite. It's a rallying cry for the leaders of innovation at legacy companies we all know and love to rethink what is possible and use their tremendous strength and power to transform the consumer marketplace for the better with radical, disruptive, and impactful innovation.

The question is, what are the startups doing right, and what can big CPG learn from them? More specifically, how can you, as an innovator in a big company, build the "fire in the machine" to harness the passion, drive, and nimbleness of small CPG and apply it to the power of big CPG?

The problem doesn't lie with front-end innovation models, creating powerful ideas, or even making it all happen through execution. Large companies have plenty of smart, talented people coming up with innovative ideas all the time and have all the resources they need to make ideas real. But when it comes to moving forward on the newest and most powerful ideas internally, especially the more disruptive ones, it's the very strengths of the large CPGs that seem to become the greatest barriers.

In most big CPG companies, there are decades of history with amazing teams creating, building, and perfecting rigorous processes designed to optimize large-scale production, consistency, and quality control. But ultimately, those exact processes are part of the challenge that can get in the way of doing something new and break through.

There are a multitude of other guardrails—each of which are appropriate and valid—that protect powerful brands, their consumers, and the employees who work on them for all the right reasons. We understand those constraints and value them, but the industry is shifting, and fast. **If big CPG doesn't find a way to be a driver of disruptive innovation that creates new categories and engages consumers, then the shift we see happening to smaller brands will continue and accelerate—driving a massive shift in power.**

QUOTE: *"The CPG Bigs have every advantage when it comes to creating innovation that delights consumers and compels retailers. Yet entrepreneurs continue to outflank and out-innovate us with their agility."*

—TODD NEWMAN,
Vice President of Innovation, Keurig Dr Pepper

When we discuss the challenges of innovation with our big CPG clients, we often hear (or read in RFPs) things like the following:

- "For a category leader, we do a lot of following. It's not sustainable leadership—we need to future proof our portfolio."

- "We do what we do really well, so we're hesitant to make changes to that expertise without proving success first. We don't have the tolerance to wait and prove things out. It either has to work ASAP or not. This is why we tend to execute line extensions or things close to our core capabilities first."

- "Our pipeline ideas often are close in and reactive (to competition, technologies, etc.). We need to find long-term opportunities that will truly be meaningful for retailers and consumers."

- "We know how to research, learn, and develop ideas to get to consumer desirability, but when a project is aimed at growing in a way that is not simply a new product, we become frozen and don't know how to execute or even model viability and feasibility—those ideas appear so risky, we can't and don't know how to move forward."

- "Our expertise has long been honed on 'say'-based research, testing the individual parts of a new proposition, but more and more our team is pushing to get to 'do'-based validation, having consumers react to the full proposition in the context of their lives. It's 'show me, don't tell me,' and as big as we are, we don't have that capability or expertise."

- "Our leadership often shifts focus and priority in a big way, practically every two to four years. Heck, we've had six layoffs in the past eight years. This change of leadership and strategy makes everyone feel rudderless—like there is no direction, and we're just writing decks to write decks."

- "On the life cycle of new category creation, we tend to enter at the proliferation stage (third of four stages) with acquisitions or brand extensions, but this may not be a viable strategy going forward as disruptive brands are being acquired earlier in the innovation life cycle, and competition for those targets is fierce. We need to learn to do this ourselves."

- "We can be slow to launch innovation projects because we fear failure, but we're also slow to kill projects, and I've watched us grind away at bad ideas for years."

- "It's amazing to think that we launch over one thousand new items a year. A lot of effort goes into all of that. Unfortunately, the vast majority of those new items are package changes, label changes, seasonal and promotional offerings—products that perpetuate what we have but don't offer anything new and exciting."

- "I have learned that if someone inside my company offers to help me produce a new innovation [for a test], I need to run away. They always mean well, but it only ends up bogging the project down once they apply the company's systems to everything."

- "Do you know how much IP we have locked up in PowerPoint decks? We have an unlimited list of 'winning' ideas at our fingertips that get recast and recycled internally about every five to eight years. Why aren't we launching these? It's probably because each one poses a level of risk, and we're just afraid of failure."

There's no doubt that the challenges to creating and driving disruptive innovation are complex, intricately interwoven, and difficult to overcome. There's no monolithic cause, nor can it be boiled down to a simple formula. On the contrary, there is a complicated array of issues at work with launching innovations, including elements like these, which we will cover in detail:

1. Managing Internal Risk Tolerances

2. Fitting Within Existing Systems

3. Prioritizing Long- versus Short-Term Horizons

4. Envisioning Possibilities

5. Striving for Perfection

6. Changing Landscapes

7. Turning Ideas into Action

All of these can become hindrances to realizing consistent, powerful, and breakthrough strategic innovation.

Fortunately, we know there is a better way. Disruptive ideas can ignite from sparks that flash with possibility and high potential and then get the space, fuel, understanding, and support to catch fire and grow—and beat the odds.

INSIGHT: According to the late Harvard Business School professor Clayton Christensen, there are over thirty thousand new products introduced every year and 95 percent of them fail. According to University of Toronto professor Inez Blackburn, the failure rate of new grocery store products is 70 to 80 percent.[2]

Academic research shows that between 70 and 95 percent of new product launches fail. And since only a small portion of ideas get launched, that means the failure rate of front-end concepts is even higher. Most CPG marketers know that if an innovation concept, no matter how unique, powerful, and category-changing it is, doesn't have line-of-sight to generate at least $25 million in the first year, it will never get past the stage-gate process inside a large CPG company—leaving hundreds or thousands of good ideas on the cutting room floor to perish without ever having a chance.

If a new idea does launch and starts off doing well but isn't working during its first ninety days at one of the key retailers, it's almost certainly going to be pulled off the shelves before the year is out. **With that kind of pressure, and the ever-present risk of significant failure, there's an internal "prove it to me" hurdle, even when the business opportunity shows long-term promise, and the project team believes in the idea.**

---

2 Marc Emmer, "95 Percent of New Products Fail. Here Are 6 Steps to Make Sure Yours Don't," *Inc.*, July 6, 2018, https://www.inc.com/marc-emmer/95-percent-of-new-products-fail-here-are-6-steps-to-make-sure-yours-dont.html.

QUOTE: *"One of the many differences I observed after moving to a startup from a large CPG company was the speed in which we made decisions. What took months or even years at the large company was often accomplished in days at the startup."*

—JULIA WING-LARSON,
Managing Director, Mission Field®

Even though entrepreneurial startups are often challenged by a lack of resources, funding, and possibly even processes, they are also free from many constraints and are able to take advantage of exciting opportunities at a blazingly fast pace. In the absence of barriers and complexity, the "little guys" are able to take much greater risks and try ideas in ways that established CPG companies simply haven't been willing or able to do. The small startups generally move, pivot, and act far more quickly, and quite frankly, they just don't give up.

Historical trends and technological developments in the last few decades have democratized the world of CPG in a way that previously would have been unimaginable, creating more opportunities for nascent companies to compete with global corporations. As a result, startups that might once have been dismissed by large companies as mere "ankle biters" have become a critical threat, and collectively, even more so.

Consider the example of craft beer in the United States in the last fifteen years. While the major beer producers still dominate the market, forty out of the fifty top breweries in the country are now craft breweries as people actively seek out small-label, premium brands.[3]

These trends aren't limited to craft beer. Indeed, a variety of factors across the CPG world—the rise of co-manufacturing, the democratization of communication, increased venture capital funding, direct-to-consumer sales access online, a shift in power toward the retailers, and many others—have created an environment in which startups have more opportunity to compete with the big players. And because of their ability to innovate quickly, they are proving to be fierce competitors to some of the largest and most profitable companies in the world.

The good news is, big consumer packaged goods manufacturers still retain numerous distinct and powerful advantages, and they *can choose* to drive innovation just like the startups. They *can choose* to take seemingly smaller and riskier bets based on consumer insight and an "informed gut." They *can choose* to make their riskiest ideas become real, and become better validated, through small-scale testing.

They *can choose* to validate key assumptions of the model with real-world data to prove out and de-risk the most disruptive and exciting ideas. Lastly, they *can choose* to harness the mindset of entrepreneurs and combine it with the power of big corporations.

---

3 Brewers Association," Brewers Association Releases the Top 50 Brewing Companies by Sales Volume for 2020," press release, March 30, 2021, https://www.brewersassociation.org/press-releases/brewers-association-releases-the-top-50-brewing-companies-by-sales-volume-for-2020/.

They *can choose* to lead category change and future proof their growth. And when they do, it is going to lead to amazing results.

CASE: Greek Yogurt—In 2006, many of the big CPG companies were working on the development of Greek yogurt as the idea had bubbled up from Europe and there was early traction from tiny FAGE, which had been imported into the US since 1998. One after another, each company dismissed it as either a niche trend that was too small of an idea, a product flavor profile that was too tart for US consumers, or a technology too difficult to make as it required different manufacturing from what US dairy producers had in their plants. Yet Hamdi Ulukaya, the founder of Chobani, believed in its potential, and his perseverance radically changed the landscape of yogurt's US grocery sales, growing from $0 to over $1.4 billion in net sales in 2021, capturing 20 percent of the entire yogurt market,[4] massively affecting the US market leaders Dannon and Yoplait, and teaching and retraining consumers that yogurt did not just have to be sweet and sugary.

A NEW PATH AND A NEW LENS

In this book, we're going to present you with a series of well-honed, tested, and validated methodologies that will give the

---

4 Michelle Cheng, "How Chobani Swallowed 20% of the US Yogurt Market," Quartz, November 18, 2021, https://qz.com/2091778/how-chobani-is-fending-off-the-competition-from-big-yogurt/.

most disruptive and risky ideas a better chance to live, breathe, and grow inside of your organization.

But first, introductions are in order.

We are Jonathan Tofel, CEO/Founder, and Carolina Sasson, COO, of Mission Field®, a fast-growing consultancy made up of former CPG executives who also have worked on entrepreneurial ventures, and this book is the result of our own learning journeys. Having spent decades in the worlds of both large, established, and powerful CPG companies *and* small CPG startups, we've seen firsthand the different strengths, weaknesses, opportunities, and challenges that each faces, particularly in regard to new product innovation. With our unique backgrounds, we've developed and refined tailored methodologies to help innovators in large companies overcome their innovation challenges, allowing them, and you, to create new paths to test, realize, and appropriately validate your most exciting and disruptive ideas.

Inside every big CPG company, extraordinarily talented team members come up with a wide spectrum of powerful innovations, renovations, and new-to-the-world ideas all the time, but many of those ideas struggle to find a path forward. Indeed, many spectacular new product concepts are buried in CPG PowerPoint decks because there simply isn't the right intuition, the right validation, or the right path to proof-of-concept that provides a large CPG with confidence about an innovation's true potential—all while balancing the risks and rewards of doing something disruptively new and breakthrough.

While a single book can't possibly address all of the specific innovation challenges you face in your organization, our goal is to offer some new ideas and additional lenses for building, testing, and de-risking disruptive innovation.

Our hope is that, in the end, you will be able to ignite the "fire in the machine" to create radical and disruptive innovation inside your company that can drive new growth in new ways. You can then use your power to transform the consumer marketplace for the better with all the quality, efficiency, and power that a big CPG company brings to the table.

PART ONE

WHY WE DO WHAT WE DO

CHAPTER ONE

EVERYTHING WE THOUGHT WE KNEW WAS AND WASN'T TRUE

"It's hard to unknow what you know."

—CAROLINA SASSON

JONATHAN'S STORY: FROM POWER AND DISCIPLINE TO THE WILD WEST

Jonathan's journey into the world of large CPG began over twenty-three years ago when he started at Procter & Gamble in brand management. At P&G, Jonathan learned how to manage and build multimillion-dollar brands with best-in-class brand building, business strategy, consumer insights, advertising development, finance, R&D development, and so much more.

He was also part of the team that developed the MDO (Market Development Organization), which embedded brand teams within the sales division to make the entire organization more effective with the end customer. He worked on growing brands, failed brands, and new possibilities. His entire experience at P&G gave him deep appreciation for the value of all the cross-functional departments and the challenging roles that they each own in keeping both hundred-million and billion-dollar brands growing and surviving.

After P&G, Jonathan jumped at the chance to do something different and took an opportunity to join a small up-and-coming CPG startup in Colorado. That company was called Orange Glo—best known for their category-disrupting brand OxiClean and their late-night direct-to-consumer infomercials. It was a much smaller company experiencing a rocket ride of success—tens of millions when he joined, growing to close to a quarter of a billion during his time there.

When Jonathan joined OxiClean, he naively assumed it would operate similarly to P&G, using the same disciplined approach but with fewer resources. He could not have been more wrong. At P&G, Jonathan had had a deep bench of talented cross-functional partners helping him do amazing things: absorbing consumer insights, analyzing complex datasets, executing world-class scientific R&D, managing a first-class sales team, and more.

However, at OxiClean, instead of finding a mini-P&G, Jonathan discovered a world that operated more on its gut and ability to pivot than on well-crafted plans and carefully thought-out strategy. Though OxiClean surprisingly lacked what felt like everything he knew before, including gaps in the cross-functional departments, data insights, and overall resources, it grew rapidly and was able to keep billion-dollar competitors at bay.

One thing he quickly noticed was that the company had a unique entrepreneurial spirit that allowed it to accomplish amazing feats. Because both strategy and research were fast and endlessly flexible, there was a prevailing attitude that said, "Go and try it *now*, no matter the risk." It was like the Wild West of CPG, and the atmosphere was full of excitement and energy. Amazingly, ideas could go from an initial spark of an idea to on-shelf in as little as six weeks—a process that at a large CPG might take as long as five years! Now, to be fair, an "on-shelf" experience might have only meant a few cases in a single hardware store, but it still showed a deference to action that amazed him then, and he has never seen it replicated since.

INSIGHT: One of the unique features of an entrepreneur is the culture of the entrepreneurial spirit. When leaders have the agency to say, "Go and try it *now*, no matter the risk," it means the organization is primed to grow because risk-taking that is both accepted and encouraged tends to uncover new and powerful possibilities, rather than always trying to find the safe route.

It was this type of entrepreneurial mindset that caused this tiny startup to crack open channels that had never been open to the major CPGs before, to create relationships with retailers that gave them advantages over much larger competitors, to pursue ideas and concepts with intense vigor and passion, and to pursue innovation efforts that consistently put billion-dollar competitors, all much better funded and resourced, on their heels.

Eventually Orange Glo started to be pursued by larger CPGs, and during that time one of the potential acquirers—the Clorox Company—recruited Jonathan to work for them as an out-of-house entrepreneur to bring a little of that OxiClean magic into their powerful multibillion-dollar organization. Jonathan updated and refined elements of the OxiClean model, adjusting it to add—and take full advantage of—the rigor and discipline that a company like Clorox requires and is capable of providing. In his time there, Jonathan was able to get disruptive innovations from their idea state (i.e., a paper concept) to the shelf in as little as six months with that same entrepreneurial spirit, but also with a highly iterative, disciplined, and supported process from an organization that wanted to grow in new ways.

Since many big companies have innovation processes and stage-gate models that can take multiple years to even be able to test a new product line, six months from idea to on-shelf was considered incredibly radical and disruptive. What amazed him while doing this was how senior leaders at Clorox always asked, "How are you doing this? How are you making these things happen so quickly and effectively?"

That is a story unto itself—essentially, the story of Mission Field®—but the big insight was that Jonathan saw a path where he could combine his entrepreneurial experiences at OxiClean with the robust resources and disciplined processes of big CPG companies like P&G and Clorox. When applied correctly, the entrepreneurial process fused with the power and resources of a large CPG is a match made in heaven!

CAROLINA'S STORY: FALLING IN LOVE WITH THE ENTREPRENEURIAL WAY

Carolina started her career at Procter & Gamble after earning her MBA from Duke's Fuqua School of Business. Like Jonathan, her experience in the FemCare division at P&G was filled with world-class marketing and brand building. It was a fast-paced and thorough education in the best of CPG.

In 2005, Carolina moved west and accepted a position at WhiteWave Foods, then a one-year-old, newly formed, sub-billion-dollar conglomerate of three category-creating brands (Horizon Organic, Silk, and International Delight) within the much bigger Dean Foods. The entire WhiteWave organization was smaller than the single FemCare division of P&G that she'd left. Carolina went from having access to every discipline and a vast amount of data to a company that felt like it was building the plane while flying it.

WhiteWave moved fast, and it was exciting. In those early days, it was still operating much like three small companies and they were decisive, with a fierce entrepreneurial spirit in everything they did. The culture was, at its core, about honoring their category creators' history. Over the next nearly eleven years at WhiteWave, she worked on all the legacy businesses, launched WhiteWave's first new brand in the US, Rachel's Wickedly Delicious yogurt and cottage cheese, drove huge growth in Club, and led the Café Nation innovation team, all while WhiteWave grew into a full-fledged big CPG company with all the complexity, layers, and bureaucracy required of a multibillion dollar organization.

During that same time period, Carolina also developed and launched a small baked goods brand outside of WhiteWave called Goodbody Baked Goods. The idea was born from her love of CrossFit and Paleo, and with a CrossFit friend, they went from idea to consumer validation, production, and launch in three months. At the time, Carolina thought that she would apply her big CPG experience to this startup, but she soon found out that the small-scale entrepreneurial venture is actually what paid her dividends in CPG as it honed her skills and built her love of the entrepreneurial way.

The hands-on experience of building her own financial models, doing her own manufacturing, leading sales pitches, arranging deliveries, and selling at the Boulder, Colorado, farmer's market was the best and richest direct research possible. This entrepreneurial experience led Carolina to be an active supporter of early-stage female food founders, where she gives her time to help others grow their ideas. She is an advisor, board member, and active in Naturally Boulder in her hometown of Boulder, Colorado.

For her last few years at WhiteWave Foods, Carolina was tapped to lead a new intrapreneurial innovation team called the Seed Group, whose goal was to drive accretive growth with new brands, channels, and targets. This skunkworks-like team of marketers and R&D launched and real-world tested dozens of SKUs and several new brands including Sir Bananas Banana-milk, Yulu, and Bonza yogurts along with creating a model to drive rapid innovation from pipeline to business-case evaluation and consumer-centric, low-cost "tests" fueled by continuous trendspotting.

> **QUOTE:** *"When I was invited to be a guest entrepreneur, I challenged the Seed Group to launch and operate like me—minimal marketing, a product that consumers can get passionate about and solves a real problem and most importantly be scrappy."*
>
> —KERRY GILMARTIN,
> Founder of four startups including Bamboobies

From P&G to WhiteWave to Goodbody, Carolina has experienced the entire spectrum of CPG over her career, from a top-tier CPG company to a very small direct-to-consumer entrepreneurial endeavor. Like Jonathan, she has seen firsthand the advantages and the challenges to innovation that companies have at all stages and all sizes, and these insights became a critical addition to the ethos of Mission Field®.

THE MISSION OF
MISSION FIELD®

So, how did we first begin working together at Mission Field®? As it turns out, we worked together during Carolina's time at White-Wave Foods. We realized we'd both had similar experiences in the world of large CPG companies and entrepreneurial startups, and we'd both been mulling the same question: **How can you apply entrepreneurial thinking to large CPG companies in order to accelerate and amplify internal innovation?**

And that's the question that drives both of us to this day and why we've continued to focus on helping large CPG clients innovate like entrepreneurs ever since.

Every day, we work with smart people in large consumer packaged goods organizations trying their best to bring disruptive innovation to life within their organization. Often they pivot, adjust, or modify their ideas in order to make something truly disruptive survive the stress testing of their internal operation.

We feel the point that should be made is this: **Why modify a disruptive idea to fit the system when the better approach is to leverage new methodologies that will help the large organization more easily digest and approve of something radically new and different?**

In the following chapters, we hope to provide additional lenses, insights, and methodologies that are less about knocking down walls, but rather provide brand-new doors, hallways, tunnels, and escape hatches that allow even the largest CPG company to comfortably create action, validation, and confidence behind some of their most disruptive opportunities.

But how did it even get this way in the first place?

CHAPTER TWO

WHY THINGS ARE
THE WAY THEY ARE

"In recent years, the leading brands in each CPG category have generated only 25 percent of value growth in US Nielsen-covered channels. Meanwhile, small and medium-sized brands captured 45 percent of the growth."[5]

—MCKINSEY & COMPANY

---

5   Udo Kopka et al., "What Got Us Here Won't Get Us There: A New Model for the Consumer Goods Industry," McKinsey & Company, July 30, 2020, https://www.mckinsey.com/industries/consumer-packaged-goods/our-insights/what-got-us-here-wont-get-us-there-a-new-model-for-the-consumer-goods-industry.

Any company that creates something new and interesting can shake up an existing category, but it has been surprising to see just how much impact small consumer products brands have had over the last couple of decades. Theoretically, big brands should have the biggest effect on any category because they have the resources, relationships, expertise, and power to make things happen, but small brands are clearly capturing some kind of magic that big brands have not yet integrated internally.

CLOSE TO HOME

Market leaders have a natural inclination to stick to doing what they do best. At the same time, there is a need for those market leaders to make improvements and changes in order to stay relevant and continue to drive growth. As a result, large CPG brands continually offer new product ideas while trying not to deviate too far from their existing core product lines—which makes a lot of sense. Would they alienate their loyal consumers by straying from the core? Would their brand begin to lack relevance with a new target audience, or would it negatively reframe the core business if they pushed into new spaces?

Imagine a sugary cereal trying to launch a Paleo (no grain, no sugar) or Keto (low carb) cereal. It's the antithesis of what the brand and much of the cereal category stands for: a sweet, grain-based, filling carbohydrate. In those situations, the innovation teams have a difficult decision to make. It's an ongoing debate about how far a brand should extend itself, how much to pivot, and whether or not the organization needs to go through the expensive and difficult task of creating a new brand to capture future growth.

The Pringles brand was a breakthrough category innovation when first launched by P&G in 1968. Rather than using slices of potato, they came up with the revolutionary idea of using potato flakes to create a unique saddle-shaped (aka hyperbolic paraboloid) structure that has a light and flavorful crunch and a wonderful in-mouth experience. Eating them is a joy, and Pringles' current owner, Kellogg's, is constantly pushing the envelope to release new flavors and varieties.

But since Pringles launched, have you ever seen any Pringles with a wildly different shape? Or a wildly different set of base ingredients? Interestingly enough, P&G "sort of" executed a major pivot like that for the first time thirty years after the brand's initial launch with a triangle shaped Pringle—the 2001 Torengo—which is no longer on the market. And as the brand manager described back then, the company "considered putting the chips under the Pringles name early on in its two and a half years of research, but decided against it."[6] Usually, once a brand establishes its distinctiveness and its purpose in the marketplace, there is a natural internal drive, an operational anchor, and a consumer conceptual framework that all make it hard to push further away from the core format that has given a brand its continued success. And as P&G learned, launching the whole new brand of Torengos was widely expensive, requiring a year-one marketing plan of "$60 million..., which includes national television and print advertising, product sampling and a direct mail program."[7]

---

6 "Procter & Gamble Serves Up Torengos Corn Chips," *Memphis Business Journal*, December 3, 2001, https://www.bizjournals.com/memphis/stories/2001/12/03/daily6. html.

7 "Procter & Gamble Serves Up Torengos Corn Chips."

The importance of that operational anchor is doubly as important if it's linked to a unique and proprietary manufacturing technology—such as making that hyperbolic paraboloid, a shape that drives love and passion among a devoted consumer base. Pringles made an impact when it initially shook up the conventions of its category, but now it is easy to assume that the brand will be strategically better off developing new and fun flavors for consumers to enjoy rather than trying to disrupt itself.

Or is it?

ENTREPRENEURIAL THINKING

Think like an entrepreneur for a moment. Your new, nascent, or unknown brand *needs* to make an impact with a disruptive product *immediately* if you want consumers to notice you in the midst of large and well-established brands that can outspend you. This requires the entrepreneur to do things very differently—and boldly—in order to break through. If you play by the rules of the category, you will have a hard time getting noticed. If you play the same game as the largest competitors, you will likely get crushed.

QUOTE: *"You can't look at the competition and say you're going to do it better. You have to look at the competition and say you're going to do it differently."*

—STEVE JOBS

When Peter Rahal founded RxBar in 2013, he "believed he had created a thing that is different and better than all the other things out there."[8] Instead of creating another protein bar for a crowded grocery store shelf, he developed a bar that used egg whites and dates as its primary ingredients, and he began selling individual boxes at CrossFit gyms.

Along with his co-founder Jared Smith, Rahal created the first batches of RxBar in his parent's basement—you can't get much more entrepreneurial than that. RxBar began small, quickly growing a fan base in careful and focused steps by being intentionally sold far away from the competitive shelf of other leading competitors like Clif, Luna, Balance Bar, and Zone Perfect to an interested and captive audience.

And what happened? In four short years, RxBar grew to $170 million in annual sales and then was purchased by Kellogg's for $600 million.[9] Looking back, there is no proprietary technology, no unique manufacturing lines, and no customized packaging—nothing specific about RxBar that Kellogg's could not have done itself.

Today, Horizon Organic is the largest producer of Organic milk in the US but back in 1991 when Mark Retzloff and Paul Repetto launched the brand, there was no established organic milk supply

---

8 Stephanie Clifford, "What Really Happens When You Become an Overnight Millionaire?" *Marker*, September 30, 2019, https://marker.medium.com/what-really-happens-when-you-become-an-overnight-millionaire-acac42990175.

9 Kellogg Company, "Kellogg Adds RXBAR, Fastest Growing U.S. Nutrition Bar Brand, to Wholesome Snacks Portfolio," press release, October 6, 2017, https://newsroom.kelloggcompany.com/2017-10-06-Kellogg-adds-RXBAR-fastest-growing-U-S-nutrition-bar-brand-to-wholesome-snacks-portfolio.

chain and the regulations—which had only just been established in 1990—required a long and costly transition period for farmers. Looking to establish and build the organic dairy business, the founders did what founders do, they focused on proving their business and consumer's desire for organic dairy products. Their entrepreneurial solution: to start in yogurt, which utilizes a lot less milk to produce a six-ounce serving than it does to produce half gallon of milk. It worked, giving Horizon Organic the time and funding they needed to get their organic milk production up to speed, at which time, they pivoted back to selling milk. With hindsight, the leading dairy companies could have made this switch. They were the ones with an existing supply chain to test and grow the idea.

The Horizon founders, just like the RxBar team, understood that they could not win by doing business like everyone else—that they had to be bold. Fundamentally, they recognized that changing consumer interests provided an opportunity, while the inherent needs of the established market leaders to grow their existing businesses gave them an opening.

Without a doubt, the challenges of starting a new brand are significant, and in order to succeed, each company had to find an entrepreneurial way to break through the market. For RxBar, it was a novel launch model through CrossFit gyms that no large CPG would even consider, the willingness to start small and grow, and their focus on a hyper-niche targeted core consumer. For Horizon Organic, it was the flexibility to pivot so as to prove the concept and consumers' willingness to pay by taking a smaller but attainable approach to entering the milk market. Both lived and breathed the entrepreneurial mindset that creates disruption.

QUOTE: *"The entrepreneurial mindset in action is someone that is willing to move forward at any cost in order to explore all the blind alleys, all the wrong turns, all the different channels, different distribution networks, different business models but staying on course in the direction that they want to develop and then testing it out."*

—GEORGE DERISO,
Professor, Entrepreneurship at University of Colorado Boulder

THE CHALLENGES OF DISRUPTION

The choice comes down to leading versus following, driving growth versus losing share, adapting versus facing irrelevance. To be clear, these are not the concerns of startups and small brands—this is a matter of concern for *all* companies. We regularly see innovation teams in companies with big brands recognize that they must push into new spaces both to drive growth and transform their categories and businesses. They know that consumer trends and the rapidly changing landscape means they *have to* innovate to keep growing and stay relevant.

The continuously changing landscape and evolving consumer desires are simply a reality that must be faced. Disruptive innovation, done by your team or the competition, has the ability to reframe entire categories with new ways of thinking about what products can and should be and who wins the hearts, minds, and wallets of the consumer. For the category leaders, it can represent a radical departure from what the category currently values and how your model operates.

For any company, breaking through the guardrails of established expectations and category norms (product, category, consumer trends, etc.) might feel very challenging—even impossible. It all boils down to risk assessment and getting away from the comfortable patterns—those natural inclinations to stick to what you know. **Disrupt yourself, or be disrupted!**

QUOTE: *"We iterated that product a few times. That's the whole point [with innovation]. Get to market as soon as possible with a viable proposition. Get consumer feedback, then tweak it. With our retail partner we told them this is version 1.0, but there will probably be a version 2.0 in a few months."*

—JOE ENS,
CEO, HighKey

One of the distinguishing features between a market-leading legacy brand and a small startup is how much each one *can pivot* and *how far* they are willing to go. There is no doubt that launching a new brand within a large organization will feel extra risky because it justifiably is. This creates an inherent bias toward launching new innovations under the powerful assets that they already possess—no matter how well they fit. This is not always the right solution for meeting the changing landscape.

What happens when an innovation team discovers that the existing brand lacks the right fundamentals to meet changing consumer desires? Launching an innovation that has the potential to turn your existing category, and your brand, on its head is very difficult to justify, support internally, and execute. It can be seen as counterintuitive and maybe even career limiting.

Imagine the challenge for an established soap company like Colgate-Palmolive's Irish Spring trying to launch a product like Dr. Squatch, which directly and purposefully tells a story that undermines the entire category of large-scale manufactured soap with their "Sh*t List," a roster of what they feel are "nasty and harmful ingredients" that Dr. Squatch vows to never use in any of their products (e.g., aluminum, parabens, phthalates, and sulfates).[10]

The same goes for shaving razors. Dollar Shave Club disrupted the "more blades" arms race that had been going on for years between Gillette, Schick, and other competitors. While the big razor companies kept adding more blades and raising prices, Dollar Shave Club upended the entire category in a heartbeat with their viral video line, "Do you think your razor needs a vibrating handle, a flashlight, a backscratcher, and ten blades? Your handsome-ass grandfather had one blade. And polio!"[11]

---

10   Dr. Squatch, "Dr. Squatch – Natural Soap for Men," May 21, 2018, video, 3:10, https://www.youtube.com/watch?v=cjEK7qQKRDY.

11   Dollar Shave Club, "DollarShaveClub.com – Our Blades Are F***ing Great," March 6, 2012, video, 1:33, https://www.youtube.com/watch?v=ZUG9qYTJMsI.

So, why are entrepreneurs and small companies more adept and willing to take on those risks and drive the disruptive growth in the industry? Why aren't the multibillion-dollar CPG manufacturers endlessly putting truly disruptive ideas on the shelf and using their power to fund and seed dozens or even hundreds of nascent ideas?

Let's look at the challenges of disruptive innovation.

QUOTE: *"The industry of consumer packaged goods is like a conveyor belt. The wheels of the belt are always slowly moving things forward. Legacy brands that don't innovate and stay relevant eventually fall off and get replaced by new upstarts with clean sheets and new visions. Those market leaders have the ability to stay on the belt if they desire, they just have to constantly work at it."*

—JOSEPH GOTTSCHALK,
President, Base3Group (and former Vice President, PepsiCo)

CHAPTER THREE

DIAGNOSING THE INNOVATION CHALLENGE

"If you want something new, you have to stop doing something old."

—PETER F. DRUCKER

DIAGNOSING A COMPLEX PROBLEM

Over the years, as we've worked with clients, we've heard our project leads express and repeat a complex array of challenges that big CPG faces when innovating.

Let's dive into seven of the most common challenges we've heard and what we've encountered directly. Bear in mind, this is not—and cannot possibly be—an exhaustive list because of the sheer complexity and variability of the situations for each business.

1. MANAGING INTERNAL RISK TOLERANCES

Newness *Feels* Risky

Anything perceived as new to an established organization system naturally feels risky. Large companies focus huge resources to operate with excellence, so while innovation teams are often pushing forward into new spaces, the rest of the organization that has to make those ideas come to life can be naturally and properly hesitant about going after anything that conflicts with their current expertise, knowledge base, or efficiency. It is the inherent bias to stick to what you do best discussed earlier, and often this means that new ideas, categories, or technologies that fall outside of current internal expertise are initially viewed with a skeptical eye.

This is most often what leads a larger CPG to focus on line extensions and ideas already close to the core. Crafting and launching something disruptive requires shaking up internal systems, processes, and gaining new expertise and manufacturing capabilities to make it work, which is always harder than doing more of the same where everyone knows what is expected. Plus, protecting the existing profitable business is important to the survival of the entity, and taking away focus or resources from the base business can have serious implications that, again, feels like big risk.

Versus

Startups generally do not have "established systems" to disrupt or big brands to protect. They are building their expertise and inherently have flexibility. Plus, everything about what they are doing is risky—every day can feel like a battle to stay alive. In that context, the need for growth through change and adaptability far outweighs the value of "doing what we've always done."

QUOTE: *"In a typical organization, some people generate ideas then let other people decide whether to go ahead with them. The decision makers are motivated by what you'd expect: how feasible something is and whether it's likely to make money, but also, and most often unconsciously, by social approval...how weird is this and how crazy am I going to look if I greenlight it?"[12]*

—JEFFREY LOEWENSTEIN,
Director, Executive MBA University of Illinois

Undifferentiated Concept Testing

Big companies utilize concept-testing tools like BASES (Booz-Allen Sales Estimating System) to determine the "potential" of new product ideas. There are multiple companies with slightly

---

12 Anne Fisher, "How Managers Accidentally Squash Innovation," *Fortune*, April 27, 2016, https://fortune.com/2016/04/27/how-managers-accidentally-squash-innovation/.

different ways of concept testing, but they all do roughly the same thing: consumers are shown a product image and written description of that concept, then they answer survey questions that help to gauge the strength of their interest in the new idea. This methodology works particularly well when you're showing consumers either a known brand, a known product benefit in a familiar category, or a previously experienced benefit. And as such, it's a great way of establishing a yardstick of success when you compare one line extension to another.

But we find that big companies often run into trouble with using concept testing when they evaluate all ideas, whether line extensions or disruptive category smashers, on the same concept-testing yardstick. Not all innovations are the same, and not all testing methodologies should be applied the same way to every innovation. We have observed time and time again with our clients how truly category-disrupting product ideas—especially products that require a consumer behavior change, a new way to perceive a category, or an experience that is hard to put into words—just do not test well in traditional concept testing. Unfortunately, we routinely watch companies deprioritizing disruptive platforms that don't have strong concept scores even though other indicators suggest they have a winner on their hands.

As a *theoretical* case study, consider how consumers might have reacted to a *written* description of kombucha before it first entered the market: "Introducing a unique, lightly effervescent sweetened fermented tea beverage that is tart and a bit sour tasting with good-for-you benefits. Note that a small cloudy mass at the bottom is a normal part of the beverage, and don't shake it as it can explode."

It likely would have sounded unpalatable and maybe a bit scary to anyone who was unfamiliar with it, even if they were open to carbonated drinks and tended toward healthy eating. Our guess is that kombucha would have failed most traditional concept-testing formats because you needed to experience it to understand it. Interestingly, numerous kombucha brands now flourish in both natural and conventional grocery stores and the *category exploded in only five years,* from $1 million in sales in 2014 to *$1.8 billion* in sales in 2019, with the total number of brands increasing by about 30 percent a year annually for the last several years.[13]

Versus

Let's start by pointing out that startups don't generally have the funding to run concept tests. They rely on direct and early live feedback rather than theoretical concept testing, thus bypassing this challenge. They must accept the risk that they do not know how their product stacks up to the industry norm. They are also most likely a believer and ground their passion in bringing a unique offering to others. No words on paper—just samples in people's mouths to get feedback.

QUOTE: *"If you see a bandwagon, it's too late."*

—JAMES GOLDSMITH

---

13 "Kombucha on the Rise," Market Watch, October 28, 2020, https://www.market-watchmag.com/kombucha-on-the-rise/.

Data as King

Some companies rely chiefly on available data about category growth or segmentation when deciding whether, where, and how they want to innovate, and to help them de-risk their overall innovation efforts. These teams often think, "If this segment is big and we see growth, then that's where we want to be with our brand." It's a top-down approach, and if pursued without both consumer and customer insights, it becomes largely hypothetical and can lead down long and winding roads of exploration that end up at dead spaces where it's ultimately determined that the brand does not have a right to win or is simply too late to the table.

We also see innovation stall behind analysis paralysis. Marketers, whose early training is steeped in brand performance analysis, get used to proving their point of view through data. It's required. As they move to innovation teams, they look for conviction through data. We often hear at kickoff meetings, "We have a great idea, but we're having trouble getting organizational buy-in on what to do next." The client then shares reams of data where they have tested, retested, and analyzed the category, platforms, and ideas repeatedly.

What we see in these scenarios is that the innovation teams often have the right gut feeling based on the correct consumer insight—it's just that they don't have the data to back it up, so the opportunity stalls out with key internal stakeholders. Maybe the challenge is they are a little ahead of the curve of consumer trends, maybe the concept just needs a little tweaking, but the need for the perfect set of data is what ends up getting them stuck with how, or if, to move forward.

Versus

Startups generally have very limited access to data and few stake-holders to convince. They read what data they can get but are not burdened by segmentations and reams of data. That means the place to look for feedback is the consumer and the place to look for trends is the internet. Plus, small hands-on teams tend to hone their gut through direct interactions. It is a double-edged sword but tends to provide the freedom to move and take action.

QUOTE: *"I've never seen a model that comes to fruition. The best companies will outperform the models, the worst companies will underperform the models. No one ever hits their model. I think there's analysis paralysis because they're all based on assumptions. So, how do you start to test assumptions without being in market? We always want people to start small, test it in a market. Once you've gotten that engine working, then scale."*

—CARLE STENMARK,
General Partner, VMG Partners

Shiny Objects and the Fear of Failure

In the marketing function of big CPG, you're rewarded with career progression for all the things you do well with your business, including launching products successfully. It can be seen as a career-limiting move to be part of a string of failures, even if you personally learn from each one and help the company improve a launch on your next assignment.

Additionally, the CPG up-or-out culture, where only the strongest marketers—often the ones who make the least mistakes—make it to the next level creates an inherent Catch-22 when it comes to innovation. If you can't afford to fail, then you're going to take smaller risks with a higher probability of success. But if you only take smaller risks, then you're less likely to create a true breakthrough innovation that company leaders are always seeking.

Even when an innovation team's culture allows risk taking and pushing boundaries, the fear of failure might still exist in other places throughout the organization, specifically within the cross-functional teams who are going to be critical to making an idea come to life, and whose own annual review is measured on different metrics like quality, consistency, and efficient throughput.

Versus

Entrepreneurs and small companies simply don't have the layers and hierarchy to face this challenge. With a singular focus and smaller teams, there tends to be alignment on what everyone needs to do to win. Plus, there is no expectation to win each wave of the work they do—it's more of a one-up, one-down roller coaster.

QUOTE: *"We're slow to launch projects because we fear failure."*

—CPG MARKETING VP

QUOTE: *"Don't be afraid of the unknown. The unknown is out there. It's identifying where there are unknowns and deciding how you're going to deal with it—if that's modeling out the answer to an unanswered question or deciding that you're going to try X, Y, and Z in order to close the gap on the unknown. Just don't be afraid of it."*

—ANNIE RYU,
CEO and Founder, the Jackfruit Company and Jack & Annie's

2. FITTING WITHIN EXISTING SYSTEMS

Manufacturing Efficiency Bias

When you have a factory that knows how to make a specific product, it's much easier to stay focused on that product and keep trying to sell more of it rather than diversifying focus or seeking a CAPEX (i.e., CAPital EXpenditure) investment that will help you create something outside of your current capabilities. Plus, there are entire teams whose focus and rewards are based on increased output, quality, and lowering the cost of manufacturing.

Even moving to external co-manufacturing is often seen as risky and outside of many companies' comfort levels as they are used to 100 percent internal ownership. Plus, we've seen it take up to two years to get a new co-manufacturer certified within our large CPG clients. And when those "new" co-manufacturers are actually businesses that have been operating for over thirty years or have global operations, the careful certification process begins to feel overly cautious at best and at worst does not support nimble innovation development.

Versus

Few startups have big-scale manufacturing. Starting relatively small with a co-manufacturer is the norm and provides forced flexibility.

QUOTE: *"It's hard for us to think outside of our own manufacturing capabilities. We simply don't have the tolerance to test out small ideas with big potential."*

—CPG VICE PRESIDENT

Managed to the Middle

Innovation teams can unintentionally undermine a powerful platform by allowing the core of an idea to get changed slowly over time in small increments—essentially, watering down the idea—with all the right intentions. This often happens as part of a linear, iterative development process where an idea is broken down to its subparts and tested in pieces (packaging, price, flavors, design, claims, etc.). Results for each piece are shared with the team, leadership, and sponsors—each of whom has a voice in the process. Small votes and changes accumulate. The final, reassembled product has often morphed significantly from the original core that made it unique. It is not unusual for us to see the final product having been managed to a middle that is safer, more mainstream, and inevitably less disruptive.

QUOTE: *"The number one thing I don't think [big companies] should do...is have everyone vote on [new product ideas] or make any decisions by committee. I think they need to empower a leader to say, "This is what we're going to do; let's go do it." And then choose the most outrageous [ideas], the ones that are most on the edge. If they do it by committee, if they water it down, when someone says, "Oh, we're going to do this one, but we'll hedge a little bit" so it's a little safer by pulling back the budget by 25 percent, or making it a little less outrageous— don't do that.*

"None of those exciting billion-dollar ideas started small. They all sounded weird as hell when the first person said them. I would run toward the weirdest ideas. I would hire teams completely outside the corporate enterprise and I would give them a lot of autonomy and tell them to go run with it. And not spend too much money on it."

—SHANE EMMETT, former CEO, Health Warrior,
and entrepreneur-in-residence, Robins School of Business,
the University of Richmond

During Carolina's time at WhiteWave, there was an idea in the Café Nation business unit with qualitative and concept testing results that were top-notch and early prototypes that were delicious and distinctive. As the idea progressed through the internal stage-gate process and at each leadership presentation, multiple stakeholders slightly adjusted and modified the idea with their own biases, business needs, or with P&L pressures on their mind. When the final product was ready for launch, it didn't resemble the initial winning concept at all.

It had slowly moved from a new food-forward brand to being part of an existing brand name. And by assigning it to that existing brand, the consumer target was broadened and became more mainstream. And to match that new target audience, the flavor profile and ingredients became known and familiar rather than innovative—all which delivered an optimized P&L that fit the needs of the larger business. While each step might have made sense as a build, it also resulted in a much more generic and nondistinct opportunity. The product eventually launched, then was discontinued within two years. We believe the original concept might have been a winning idea if it was able to maintain the core elements of where it initially started.

Versus

Startups generally don't have a middle to manage to. The teams are small, and the product and consumer drives everything. Plus, founders who lead the business are passionate about their idea—it's why they are giving it everything to have it grow.

Battleships versus Speedboats

Large CPG companies are excellent when launching a new brand at making millions of units of a product and distributing it throughout the country in a matter of months. The average consumer may not understand or appreciate this, but the way a CPG company can make that happen is an amazing feat of human engineering and logistics. It's part of what makes category-leading brands powerful in their own right. But it also comes with a downside. When your operations are designed for national launches achieving 85 percent ACV (all commodity volume) in a matter of months, they naturally struggle with anything that might be smaller and more nimble. In fact, making five hundred or five thousand units of a new-to-the-world idea can be *almost as complex* as making a million units within the same company.

The analogy often used inside large CPG companies is that they are like a battleship—a large and powerful force to be reckoned with, but one that also moves slowly and can't turn on a dime. In competitive reviews, we often hear our clients describe nascent brands with a mix of curiosity, amazement, wonder, and a dash of jealousy—they wish they could act like them, but they can't.

Naturally, this scale versus speed structure tends to negate or challenge the ability for a large company to place a lot of small bets and see how they rise to the top. Instead, they are mostly locked into a model that is an all-or-nothing launch format—one that is well-designed for their systems and ways of operating, but also reduces their ability to act quickly and nimbly to growing trends and opportunities.

Versus

Entrepreneurial brands are more like speedboats. They are small, fast, and zoom all over the place in a way a battleship can't. Speed is one of their distinct advantages by virtue of size, limited layers, and survival urgency.

QUOTE: *"I've long believed that speed is the ultimate weapon in business. All else being equal, the fastest company in any market will win. Speed is a defining characteristic—if not the defining characteristic—of the leader in virtually every industry you look at. This is how category killers are made."*

—DAVE GIROUARD,
CEO of personal finance startup Upstart,
and former President of Google Enterprise Apps[14]

---

3. PRIORITIZING SHORT- VERSUS LONG-TERM HORIZONS

Success Expectations

Generally, big CPG companies have an expectation that new product launches have to hit big numbers quickly. For most

---

14 Dave Girouard, "Speed as a Habit," First Round Review, accessed June 28, 2022, https://review.firstround.com/speed-as-a-habit.

organizations this falls somewhere between $25 and $50 million in sales in year one. Because of that base hurdle rate, it's much harder, and rarer, to find internal support for a launch that starts at $1 to $5 million (much less $100,000) and *has the potential* to build to a larger size, say $150 million, over a longer period of time, like RxBar. Smaller launches create their own risks in that they will likely become a negative drain on the P&L in the short term, they have no guarantee of success (remember the failure rates), and big CPGs are not set up to do anything small scale. In an odd way, it is often easier to have the machine of a large CPG deliver full national distribution than it is to execute a launch starting in three hundred CrossFit gyms. By default this often creates internal hurdles around "emerging category" opportunities.

Naturally, with these internal hurdles and large launch focuses, innovation within big CPG companies ends up being an all-or-nothing scenario.

Versus

Every entrepreneur starts with zero sales and only dreams of reaching the heights of what the big CPG companies expect for a national launch in terms of years not months. Horizons are naturally close in, and expectations are on a step-by-step growth plan.

CASE: *Jumping into an Emerging Category*—"When we were trying to launch the SToK Cold Brew Coffee brand, we were asked by leadership, 'Why would we want to be a part of a tiny $10 million dollar category?' Even though we had a strong gut feeling that the third wave coffee trend was about ready to explode, there was financial and personal risk of leaning into a small category and projecting the $250+ million category over time. We [luckily] passionately proved our business case internally, and positioned the brand to drive the category growth versus the traditional wait-and-see approach."

—MJ TAVELLA, former Vice President of Marketing and Innovation, WhiteWave Foods

Note: The cold brew coffee category (both packaged products and beverages sold from coffee shops) is now projected to be just under $1 billion in sales by 2025.[15]

Limited Resources

Even though big CPG companies have the resources to develop many ideas, the company still must prioritize one opportunity over another—they simply can't tackle every new project of interest. Limited resources, the reality of the P&L, and the need to deliver consistent quarterly results tends to make large CPG companies give priority to projects that are most easily realized today with the least risk.

---

15 M. Ridder, "Cold Brew Coffee Market Value in the U.S. 2015–2025," Statista, January 13, 2022, https://www.statista.com/statistics/659724/cold-brew-coffee-sales-us/.

Versus

While this is a shared pain point where startups are even more resource constrained and must prioritize as they build, startups end up throwing everything they have into each opportunity and then quickly stop and readjust when that opportunity is not proving itself out.

QUOTE: *"The efforts spent prioritizing resources and determining which new products should get to market was a constant tug-of-war when I worked at a big CPG. The winners were always the ones that came with the most resources, not necessarily the best ideas."*

—JULIE BECK,

Managing Director, Mission Field®

No Patience

With complex annual planning cycles and expectations to meet, each launch must prove itself out according to detailed plans built by a wide group of stakeholders. Between scale efficiency needs and retailer expectations, it's much harder to *wait* for an idea to prove itself out, or to iterate and improve upon it, than it is to cut one's losses and move on to the next priority. Plus, there is scrutiny and data that is reviewed with high frequency and urgency to stay on track.

We often hear our big CPG clients reference innovative, successful startups like Justin's Nut Butters, RxBar, or IZZE when they talk about being smaller and more nimble to drive growth. But nearly all fail to account for the "quiet years" before these brands became household names. There are very few "overnight" success stories, and it's not helpful to tell your large CPG stakeholders that it took five to fifteen years to get to the place where these brands became noteworthy.

Versus

Interestingly, this is the opposite of what entrepreneurs often do, where they not only have the dedication to stick with it through those lean and hard moments, but also give their ideas the time they need to flourish and develop.

CASE: *Slow Growth of Justin's Nut Butters*—As Justin Gold, founder of Justin's Nut Butters, said about the early years of his startup, "I wasn't making enough profit margin, I wasn't in enough stores, and I was still waiting tables, *and it was really a fun activity for me.*"[16] He didn't

---

16 Stephen J. Bronner, "How Curiosity Propelled the Entrepreneur Behind Justin's to Grow a $100 Million Brand," *Entrepreneur*, May 14, 2018, https://www.entrepreneur.com/article/312855.

make much money right out of the gate, but he was able to have patience for a couple of years as he built grassroots loyalty for his product, starting at the Boulder Farmers Market every Saturday. This small start eventually translated into national success and an eventual lucrative acquisition by Hormel.

Justin started the brand in 2004 and sold it in 2016—it was a twelve-year success story.

External Pressures

Without dispute, the senior directors, VPs, and EVPs that we interact with are incredibly talented people, amazing leaders, and adept at navigating their company's systems. However, publicly owned CPGs also have another set of priorities, and long-term innovation isn't often going to be the primary focus when Wall Street demands to see growth in revenue and profit on a quarterly basis. A publicly traded company has to *constantly manage* growth and profitability, so the upper-level leaders have a natural inclination to spend less time and resources investing in an idea that is three, five, or seven years from being able to impact their P&L in a meaningful way.

Now, almost all Fortune 500 CPG manufacturers have long-term disruptive innovation teams that are tasked to go and uncover "further out" opportunities that the base innovation teams can't spend time on, but still, we have seen over and over again how those long-term teams bring back big ideas to their operational P&L owners only to hear, "How big is it?" "Why are we working on this?" or "How can you be certain?"

Versus

This simply does not impact startups.

QUOTE: *"We're constantly focused on the here and now, and we've been running so hard and so fast to keep up with the changes in our industry that we haven't taken a moment to pause and look five to ten years in the future."*

—CPG INNOVATION DIRECTOR

---

4. ENVISIONING POSSIBILITIES

Small-Box versus Big-Box Thinking

Different companies look at innovation through very different lenses—and often that can lead to blind spots. For example, some focus on their design and creative packaging but miss on the product. Others are focused on what's inside and pay less attention to the communication and ethos of the idea. Some are chiefly focused on trying to get their brands into new spaces regardless of the appropriateness of the fit, and others are laser-focused on their *why* and get stuck overthinking their product's purposeful anchor to the space they are in today.

As an example, we helped execute an in-market test for a client whose internal team developed a leading-edge and interesting product. The food inside the packaging was good, and the core idea was strong. But when the design team created the packaging, they worked off big monitors and focused on beautiful details on small labels. They looked amazing in a PowerPoint deck. Once the product got into real-life testing, it became 100 percent clear that the design was too small, too detailed, too precious, and consumers could not tell what it was.

The point is to not get stuck in small-box thinking. Sometimes this is referred to as "talking to ourselves," where the team gets caught up in internal dialogue and discussions. Instead, the goal is to use a big-box mindset—get many external views, take your mock-ups out of the building at real scale into real stores, talk to unbiased consumers, and maybe set up quick real-life testing to see what you might otherwise miss if you stay in the constraints of the building so as to uncover any blind spots.

Versus

This is a challenge also faced by startups, maybe even more so. Founders who relate to being the core consumer have a strong bias and blind spots that can limit their 360 review of options. They too benefit from external points of view—most often resolved through hands-on interactions (like Justin at the Farmers Market every Saturday or RxBar talking to CrossFit members).

QUOTE: *"We dedicated time to root cause analysis—why are some [new products] failing? One of the things that showed up for us is we didn't have enough touch points up front. We were relying on three guys' (founders') point of view. So, we implemented panels—they are very informal but now we get twelve or fifty data points as opposed to two or three. When you're moving at our pace, you can overlook those things."*

—JOE ENS,
CEO, HighKey

Rotating Leadership and Making it "Your Own"

Marketing managers in most CPG companies are viewed as eventual leaders of the organization, which is one reason why they are moved between brands and categories every eighteen months to two years. It makes good sense to give growing leaders many different experiences that they can apply across future assignments. However, it means a leader who is championing an idea may be shuffled off their brand, category, or division before the innovation can be finalized or readied for a commercial launch. The next leader who takes over often will want to put their own stamp on their new workflow to make their mark. Also, layoffs and reorganizations have a big impact, which can create additional instability for long-term innovation projects.

Carolina experienced this firsthand as an innovation brand manager. She was rotated onto the business as part of the normal marketing process of providing growth opportunities and career expansion. The assignment ended up lasting just nine months as a new opportunity that was a perfect fit became available. In that time she had created a three-year pipeline based on mining historical documents, executing research on brand stretch, and diving into whitespace. Just weeks after this foundational work, she moved off, and a new brand manager stepped in who would need to reevaluate the just-presented plan and make it his own.

Versus

This isn't a problem with a founder and a small team.

QUOTE: *"When I worked at a large company, the person who had the most passion and intuition for the idea often rotated off the business or wasn't on the team in charge of commercialization by the time it launched. Because of this, the true north and the spark of the idea was often lost. When I was launching new products at a startup, the same people who were making samples in the kitchen and creating the product were the ones who were writing the copy, designing the packaging, and bringing the final product to life. There was no separation between the person who birthed the idea and the person who helped it grow into something bigger, which made it stronger."*

—JULIA WING-LARSON,
Managing Director, Mission Field®

45

Lack of Ownership

There can be a lack of clarity about who owns the responsibility for innovation, especially when it comes to risky projects. Also, ideas that cross internal or retailer boundaries or ones that are championed by brand-agnostic innovation teams can be hard to have clarity of ownership. Understandably, lacking a clear champion, it is far more likely that great ideas won't be realized.

Jonathan experienced this directly when he was client side and delivered a $154 million year-one, BASES-2 tested, and test-market validated idea to his leadership. Because the idea and its list of products crossed three different categories with its assortment of six SKUs, the executive VP of each division pushed back about who was responsible for owning the project. They each wanted the revenue but not the cost of launching it, *and* they had other competing priorities on their plates that were bigger than their one-sixth portion of the projected revenue (i.e., a division VP's $50 million launch ranked as more important than having a one-sixth share or $25 million of a $150 million idea). In part, since no one stuck their neck out to resolve the internal challenges and move the project forward for the greater good of the company, it died on the vine and remains stuck in a PowerPoint deck to this day.

Additionally, many companies have breakthrough innovation teams charged with future growth that are brand agnostic to start. The transition of those ideas into one or potentially more brands can present challenges in launch success.

Versus

This does not apply to small companies with smaller teams.

QUOTE: *"Our lack of leadership (and a stakeholder) on this strategy makes us feel rudderless. Sometimes, it seems like we're writing decks just to write decks even though they keep proving the same points."*

—CPG INNOVATION MANAGER

Internal Knowledge

At times we see our clients get stuck behind their own existing knowledge base about what can and can't be done. For example, we have recently had conversations with three different clients in which the insight from consumers recommended putting their products into recyclable glass packaging, and all three clients had strong reactions against the idea because it went against their historical methodologies and knowledge. We would hear comments like, "We can't use glass; it will shatter. It's a hazard. The freight guys won't like it because it's too heavy. It's too expensive, and we'll never make money on it." Yet we know glass packaging is perfectly viable and used by many companies.

Harvest Snaps is an example that is often referenced by our clients when exploring better-for-you chip alternative snacks.

The industry knowledge points to the produce section being a suboptimal placement for this type of product. Yet Harvest Snaps has proven a viable, substantial business and trained consumers to find them where they are—far from the other chips and salty snacks.

Versus

Small companies often don't know what the industry norms are and develop new models or solutions out of necessity—without realizing what everyone else thought was impossible.

CASE: *Perfect Bar*—The story of the Keith family banding together to make their dying dad's recipe into Perfect Bars is a story worth hearing. The key point we want to focus on is that they were outsiders to the CPG world and even the natural foods industry in 2005 when the eldest twenty-two and nineteen-year-old kids started the family business. Their dad's recipe was created at home for his thirteen children and was therefore preservative free. What that meant for scaling the product to sell is that it needed refrigeration, and anyone and everyone in CPG knew it would be impossible to get precious refrigerated space dedicated to a product that is normally shelf stable. Through hard work, perseverance, and a bit of luck, they got a thirty-day trial at Whole Foods in Berkeley. As Bill Keith said, "That was the match that started the wildfire." It is reasonable to say that no big CPG company would have dreamed or persevered to break the category norm—to push for refrigeration on a normally shelf stable product and to build a successful bar business when often placed next to milk or yogurt. It took the Keith kids ten years before they got a large infusion of capital from VMG, and it was in their fourteenth year that Mondelez purchased a majority stake for an undisclosed sum.

5. STRIVING FOR PERFECTION

Pivoting and Adapting

Due to the size, risk, resources dedicated, complexity, and expectations of new product launches, large companies are motivated to make sure that everything is "perfect" prior to a launch. To their credit, an enormous amount of time and effort has gone into all the details before the "go" date. But what that means is that the work to catch and correct mistakes has to happen prior to the real, in-market sales beginning, and the ability to learn, react, and adapt postlaunch is limited, *if any.* We rarely see a process by which a large CPG has a postlaunch adaptation plan in place to pivot once it hits the store shelves. This situation is only amplified by retailers who want products to sell out of the gate. They track the data and don't generally have a process in place to account for or allow the manufacturer to pivot without penalties. The most common penalty is discontinuation.

Versus

Given a small size launch and building distribution, small companies pivot as they learn. Each new distribution expansion allows small tweaks with smaller consequences because of their smaller footprint.

QUOTE: *"If I look back and say, 'What would I change?' I would have launched much sooner with prototypes or just something to get me on-shelf sooner. I think I tried to make it perfect, but we don't really know what perfection is. Immediately when I put it on-shelf, I saw that the package didn't work. It was not sticking out. We were getting great reception on the product, but we found out that we didn't have enough variety. It took us another year to iterate on the package, launch new flavors, and get to a portfolio that was interesting to retailers."*

—SHIBANI BALUJA,
Founder and CEO, Lil' Gourmets

Holistic versus Discrete Testing

One way that innovation teams strive for perfection is to test the heck out of everything—over and over and over again. After an innovative concept has been developed they will run (in a range of various sequences) a concept test, pricing study, packaging study, sensory test, in-home use test (IHUT), switching analysis, and so on. Sometimes these studies are layered on top of one another, and the insights from one don't have a chance to impact the next. While the insights from each study are always interesting and helpful, the problem with this process is that they aren't studying the comprehensive whole of the proposition.

Versus

Small companies don't have the budgets or luxury of time to test and retest their ideas. The pace of growth, lower risk profile of their product launches, and their smaller team structures allow for internal decisions that don't force the dissection of the concept.

CASE: *Testing the Pieces, Not the Whole*—We once watched a marketing director at a large CPG company get tasked with reinvigorating an older line of haircare products that had been struggling and needed to recapture its relevance. This product line, branded with the name of a famous hairstylist—a "stylist to the stars"—should have been doing much better, as new premium entrants kept entering the category and expanding the premium subcategory around the brand. It was already considered upscale, and the stylist was a well-known household name. This was a great equity and anchor from which to start a renovation project.

The insights the team collected eventually led the director to reframe the brand to give consumers a "complete salon experience" in their homes.

So, what are the shampoo bottles like in a salon? They are premium in every way you can imagine. The formula, the scent, the design, the color, the way they work, everything. And the best way to prove that these changes will be successful? Consumer testing. The first thing tackled was the formula—upgraded to give a better experience. The director had to be *absolutely sure* that consumers would go for this, so they tested consumer reactions to the new formula with in-home research. Consumers loved it!

Then the design agency came with a request. They wanted to deviate from the brand's traditional color scheme. Instead of the bright color that the brand had been using for decades, they recommended going with black. "It's a much more premium color," they said. Just to be safe, the director tested the new color with consumers. They loved it!

Also, shampoo and conditioner bottles in the salon use pumps instead of toggle-top lids. Flip-top lids are used on the cheaper brands like Suave, so a pump would be a better way to bring the salon experience home. That was also tested and approved.

Each step of the way, the director and the team tested each possible change. The new formula had a higher cost, so the team shrank the bottle to get a better profit margin, but testing showed this would also work fine. When someone suggested labeling the bottle with the initials of the brand instead of the whole name, it was tested with consumers. Each time, they approved.

The updated and upgraded product was launched. Expectations were high. And while the marketing support announcing the launch was thinned out to support a quarterly earnings call, the team still had high hopes.

Within a few weeks of hitting the store shelves, sales volume fell by 20 percent. A month or two later, there was another 15 percent decrease. What happened? Simply put, the discrete *testing* of each variable was accurate—but only to a point. Consumers did love the changes when they saw them in isolation, in a focus-group room, but it was only when everything was put together and placed on a store shelf that the full impact would be known.

The combined color change and name change meant loyal consumers couldn't easily find it on-shelf in the sea of two hundred-plus other haircare options, so they chose one of their many other favorite brands. This led to the first sales drop. The change from the toggle to the pump led to the second drop because while consumers liked the pump, they also used 25 percent less product than the pour that came out of the toggle, which extended their need to come back and buy another bottle, effectively lengthening the repeat rate and reducing overall volume. It should come as no surprise that there was no celebration in the halls. On the contrary, there were difficult meetings and an angry celebrity stylist to contend with.

6. CHANGING LANDSCAPES

End of Mass Launches

A hypertargeted idea based on a focused consumer insight might be powerful and lead to an ideal "design target" delivery, but a big company still needs to have that idea work at Walmart and be profitable enough to justify the investment. Big companies are operationalized for scale and generally need mass launches to be successful, but mass launches are increasingly becoming more difficult and can be challenging to execute with a hypertargeted idea.

Versus

Small brands have their niche ideas survive because they can more readily endure slow growth and slim profit margins for an extended period of time to let their innovations gain a following before they ever need to get onto a Walmart shelf.

Shelf Space Pressures

The vast majority (more than 90 percent)[17] of packaged-food purchasing happens in a brick-and-mortar store like a grocery store. Within that physical location, every linear inch of shelf space is precious—and the shelf space is treated by the retailer

---

17   Russell Redman, "E-commerce to Account for 20% of U.S. Grocery Market by 2026," Supermarket News, October 22, 2021, https://www.supermarketnews.com/online-retail/e-commerce-account-20-us-grocery-market-2026.

just like a real estate agent treats a bidding war on a hot property. It's anyone's game to win the prize and nothing is guaranteed. Because of this dynamic, CPG manufacturers have to manage a very important and delicate relationship with the retail chains it uses to sell its products. Not only do manufacturers have extra pressure on them to make sure that every innovation launches perfectly, there is also the reality that retailers have the real power over what innovations they accept and make it to the shelf. If a manufacturer makes a series of misses in a row, then it's less likely that the next innovation is going to get the shelf space it needs.

Versus

The retail relationship is just as important to startups, but they are often given significantly more leeway as retailers support smaller risks and bet on future growth.

Established Buyer Relationships

Each CPG company has entrenched sales teams who build relationships with buyers who are decision-makers for their categories. If a new product is outside of their current categories, it often requires additional sales resources to call on a new set of buyers, which poses an internal challenge. Even when consumers say they would expect to see a new innovation in a specific category, we have seen our clients either force their innovations into the aisle where they already have relationships or give up on the idea altogether.

Versus

Startups face a different challenge that is less about their footprint and more about how hard it is to sell in an established placement. They are often at the mercy of the buyer to determine where the product will ultimately be placed.

QUOTE: *"Time and time again, we've run successful test markets of disruptive new products in categories where the consumer and retailer expect to find the product. Yet, when it comes time to launch, the manufacturer is confronted with the reality that their sales team isn't structured to support the new product in a new category with a new buyer. What happens next is the tragedy: typically they force fit the product into their current 'managed' categories and many times, the products don't survive."*

—JULIE BECK,
Managing Director, Mission Field®,
and thirty-year veteran of CPG sales

---

7. TURNING IDEAS INTO ACTION

Ideas Are Plentiful, Execution Is Key

New innovations ideas are abundant—even amazing, transformational breakthrough ideas—but ideas are easy. Making them come to life is the hard part. While there's no data to know how many concepts turn into real product launches, from our own experience, we've seen that for every hundred ideas that get created, maybe six to eight will make it through the validation process with consumer work and get elevated for quantitative testing. Of those, about half come back with results that signal they are worth additional energy.

What happens to those three or four good ideas? Simply put, we've seen some amazing ideas that were consumer validated multiple times in multiple ways plus were supported with passion by internal teams never progress to the next step because the path to making them come to life required a huge amount of external support, which in the end made it harder than expected to execute.

Versus

Startups have a bias toward action because they have to bring new ideas to life and find that new way to make something happen. If they can't execute their idea, they simply will not exist.

QUOTE: *"Risk is not in the conceptualization of an idea, but in the execution. That's when the money is on the line."*

—CPG PRESIDENT

Theory versus Action

There is no lack of theories, strategies, and insight approaches in the world of CPG (e.g., Blue Ocean Strategies, Jobs to be Done, Ten Types of Innovation, Crossing the Chasm, lean business models, etc.), but it's not always obvious how these bits of knowledge translate into specific action for your specific product line. We had a prospective client who makes canned products lament in an RFP discussion with us that they just didn't know what to do with all of their insights and information. They had been thinking about their innovation possibilities and challenges for such a long time—and obtained reams of data and insight decks that presented various theories on where they should go—that it became increasingly difficult to make anything happen.

Versus

Startups are not burdened by reams of data, which frees them from the analysis paralysis that can come from so much research. Though they are flying blind without the data, it can be liberating and enable a faster-paced decision-making process.

INSIGHT: The difference between an entrepreneur and a great marketer with an idea is the *bias for action*. The doing is what makes you a founder.

> **QUOTE:** *"We have tons of theoretical insights, and insights about consumer trends, but we don't actually know how they apply to our main products and our brands."*
>
> —CPG INNOVATION DIRECTOR

Here is a recap of the seven most common challenges to leading disruptive innovation:

1. Managing Internal Risk Tolerances

- New *Feels* Risky

- Undifferentiated Concept Testing

- Data as King

- Shiny Objects and the Fear of Failure

2. Fitting Within Existing Systems

- Manufacturing Efficiency Bias

- Managed to the Middle

- Battleships versus Speedboats

3. Prioritizing Short- versus Long-Term Horizons

- Success Expectations

- Limited Resources

- No Patience

- External Pressures

4. Envisioning Possibilities

- Small-Box versus Big-Box Thinking

- Rotating Leadership and Making it "Your Own"

- Lack of Ownership

- Internal Knowledge

5. Striving for Perfection

- Pivoting and Adapting

- Holistic versus Discrete Testing

6. Changing Landscapes

- End of Mass Launches

- Retailer Pressures

- Established Footprint

7. Turning Ideas Into Action

- Ideas Are Plentiful, Execution Is Key

- Theory versus Action

THE STRUGGLE IS REAL

As we said, this list of innovation challenges isn't exhaustive, nor could it be, and we're only skimming the surface of some very complex issues. However, there's a good chance that many of them resonate with your own experiences. These challenges are fairly common in large CPG, so you need to realize that your innovation struggles are real. The ideas you have championed in the past, still have heart for, but have not made progress on—the lack of progress *isn't your fault.*

Our unique experience behind the scenes in both the entrepreneurial CPG and Fortune 500 CPG worlds has shown us how common these innovation challenges are to companies of all sizes, even though leaders tend to feel like they're all alone on an island, facing these challenges by themselves. Yes, you have some real problems, but they are common to the world of big CPG, and the good news is, there are ways to get around each and every one of them.

There's no single "right" theory when it comes to innovation. As an innovator in a big CPG company, you clearly do many things incredibly well, but you might be so focused on working within the system of what you *can* do that it's possible you haven't spent as much time thinking about other ways you *could* do innovation.

Some of the challenges in this chapter aren't things you can't necessarily change—even if they hinder innovation, they are important to the company for other reasons. For example, having efficient factories that know how to create your existing products with perfection is good, even if it creates a hindrance for innovating outside of your current product portfolio. Shuffling leaders around to give them broad experience with numerous brands is important as a way to grow internal capabilities, even if it means some compelling ideas get lost in the shuffle.

Is it possible to overcome these innovation challenges without damaging the systems that currently work well in your company? It's a fair question, and we'll try to provide some perspective on this in the next chapter.

CHAPTER FOUR

IS IT EVEN POSSIBLE
TO FLIP THE SCRIPT?

"There is always a better way."

—THOMAS A. EDISON

Is it possible for innovation teams within big CPG companies to act upon their most disruptive ideas like entrepreneurs, without being hindered by the complex array of challenges? Is it really possible to flip the script?

During our time with Mission Field®, we've seen numerous companies start, energize, then collapse innovation groups over and over again. We've seen some not-so-great starts, and we've seen some very good attempts. We've seen innovation groups that continued to move forward, others that struggled within the constraints of their organizations, and many that lost support and withered away.

Along the way, we've encountered various models for innovation teams.

MODELS FOR INNOVATION TEAMS

There is no single right way to create innovation inside of a large organization. Every company has its own culture, approach, and team dynamics, so it's natural for different companies to try different models and approaches to innovation. That being said, we have seen recurring patterns in innovation teams that have their own stories to tell. Let's take a look at a few common examples and see what we can glean from their experiences.

Approaches That Have Repeatedly Struggled within Big CPG

A Place of Their Own

This model of innovation usually starts when a senior leader champions a new innovation vision, often with a long-range plan of developing ideas five to seven years out with a focus on building new categories or reaching new consumer targets. That senior leader often adopts the point of view that the base organization is either not innovative enough to support the team's objectives, or the constraints of the entire operation will slow innovation down and create unnecessary guardrails.

To address this, they pull key cross-functional people out of their traditional company assignments and give them full autonomy to pursue their new innovation goals. Often they move the innovation team to a different location separated from the main headquarters. The team gets the benefit of having multiyear assignments with the resources they need to focus on long-term innovation efforts.

At first glance, you might think this model would work well, but in every instance where we've seen it tried, these "departed" innovation teams struggled not with the ability to come up with breakthrough ideas or to test and validate them, but with translating the importance of those opportunities back into the organization. Why? Because in each case, the desire to free the team from the constraints of the organization led to a situation where they also became disconnected. Disconnected from the base brand's main goals, disconnected from annual planning, disconnected from the ever-shifting winds of strategy and focus, and sometimes even disconnected from the company culture (which caused them to be looked at quizzically by the rest of the company).

Whenever they tried to pass their validated ideas back into the heart of the company, the organization saw them as outside efforts that were "not made here," didn't fit with the current business teams' priorities, and often were too small to warrant full support without the patience to grow and build. Consequently, even with plenty of resources, autonomy, and a long-term vision, they just couldn't get enough support for their ideas.

QUOTE: *"Innovation teams [often] feel a hostility towards the people responsible for day-to-day operations...The rich vocabulary of disdain includes bureaucratic, robotic, rigid, ossified, staid, dull, decaying, controlling, patronizing...and just plain old. Such animosity explains why most executives believe that any significant innovation initiative requires a team that is separate and isolated from the rest of the company. But that conventional wisdom is worse than simpleminded. It is flat wrong. Isolation may neutralize infighting, but it also neuters innovation."*

—GOVINDARAJAN AND TRIMBLE,
Harvard Business Review[18]

The Enlightened Intrapreneurs

There are several types of models in this ecosphere that seem to pop up when a business leader feels a radical departure from the base organization is required to move innovation forward. So rather than giving an innovation team a place of their own, the leader pushes even further and tries to *teach* the people in their organization how to be more entrepreneurial. Now, on its surface,

---

18 Vijay Govindarajan and Chris Trimble, "Stop the Innovation Wars," *Harvard Business Review Magazine*, July–August 2010, https://hbr.org/2010/07/stop-the-innovation-wars.

this seems like a good thing. Large manufacturers often self-declare that they are "learning organizations" that want to keep their marketers and innovators knowledgeable about the latest insights and disruptive thinking. So teaching your staff how to be more entrepreneurial seems like an appropriate and natural extension.

When this is eventually brought to life, we have seen it manifest in many diverse ways, including: (1) sending a team from the Midwest to the San Francisco Bay area to share a rental house and collectively "live the life" of an entrepreneur for a few months—all while striving to come up with ideas and executions of new innovations, (2) training sessions from outside consultants that attempt to turn an existing staff into intrapreneurial subgroups, teaching them how to act and think differently inside their core organization, and even (3) bringing in nonindustry (often technology or an unrelated category) entrepreneurs who've had success outside the company and are now embedded in the main organization to help give a spark of those creative juices to the base organization.

Unfortunately, in each of these scenarios, we keep seeing the same results. It starts off great when the excitement and passion around the new model invigorates, inspires, and helps the team get very good at absorbing new lenses and new perspectives. As they absorb these new ways of thinking, they end up succeeding at the opportunity identification process and start to bring in ideas that the core organization would rarely, if ever, come up with on their own. Unfortunately, in each example, the process then seems to fall apart when it comes time to make those ideas real (e.g., executing them in-market and building the idea into a business that the organization would value and consider launching).

Why is this the case? It seems that these models never address the root of the problem: the main organization still has its internal inertia and focuses on doing what it knows how to do best while looking at external ideas with a bit of healthy skepticism. So no matter what cool new ideas get developed from these other sources, they run up against the wall of preferences the main organization tends to stick with over time.

QUOTE: *"Challenges for organizations to simulate intrapreneurial activities remain largely unchanged over the past decades. For example, large organizations usually are not appropriate environments to nurture intrapreneurship...Likewise, contention between employee and the managerial level signifies a primary reason why many intrapreneurs leave the organizations and start their own businesses."*

—LAN-YING HUANG, SHU-MIN YANG LIN, AND YING-JUIN HSIEH, Frontiers in Psychology[19]

The Herders

Another model we've seen tried is based on solving for continuity. Ideas that are born in the breakthrough innovation teams (whether inside or outside of the main company) are developed,

---

19   Lan-Ying Huang, Shu-Min Yang Lin, and Ying-Jiun Hsieh, "Cultivation of Intrapreneurship: A Framework and Challenges," *Frontiers in Psychology* 18 (October 2021), https://doi.org/10.3389/fpsyg.2021.731990.

tested, and set up through a prelaunch phase, often with detailed execution planning and readiness. Then one or more of the innovation team follows that innovation back into the main organization under the wing of an existing brand and its P&L. In principle, this also seems like a winning design, since you're bringing along the marketer, with all of their insight and passion, to keep giving the project life and energy and continuity.

It should be an amazing model, and there have been books written about this approach. So what is the problem? Where this design seems to fall apart is usually with the transitioning people. When you consider the rotational assignments of people in large consumer packaged goods, it's important to remember that (1) not every marketer is cut out to be an innovator, (2) the marketer's best fit for the innovation design may not be the best fit for launch and execution, and (3) the marketer may be too junior to truly affect change and lobby for the innovation within the base team.

When we've seen this model take shape, the best innovators kick things off, but within a few years, they are rotated out of the innovation group as they follow their key projects. The breakthrough innovation team becomes limited in what it can work on as they have to be able to lose a key player every time they succeed. Importantly, when a successful idea gets rolled back into the organization, the innovator that came with it typically finds that their project is just a small part of the base brand's P&L, and the idea they may have spent two to three years on gets relegated to a lower priority than it may deserve.

The Scrappy Innovators

We've seen examples of innovation teams that were purposefully underfunded so they were forced to become scrappy innovation teams modeled after cash-strapped entrepreneurs. The supporting thesis is that by not giving these teams large budgets, they would not tax the organization with too many resources or financial support and have more freedom to think in wild and disruptive ways. However, starting an innovation team with limited funding while also keeping the company's internal evaluation guardrails in place (requiring that they prove things *to the same standard* of every other brand team inside the company) makes it almost impossible to prove anything.

We've seen these scrappy teams run up against the internal standards for what it takes to prove an idea, demanding more resources than the team has access to. After all, it's one thing to do a gut check on something, but conducting qualitative work, focus groups, R&D development, and manufacturing alignment can get very expensive. If you can't afford to test and build your ideas in the way that the "mother ship" needs for validation, then the main organization will most likely say, "You didn't prove it *enough*," and the idea will die on the vine. The entrepreneurial "gut" is not an approved process for success and resource allocation, nor should it be in any big CPG company.

INSIGHT: Silicon Valley was one of the major contributors to the scrappy "fail fast" approach. In their world, designing and delivering a beta version of a piece of software and then continually improving upon the user experience is an ideal balance of scrappy innovation that can be backed by clear and compelling data. Unfortunately this is a little harder to implement when it comes to tangible consumer products that require R&D, prototypes, and logistics. Unless one reframes what level of insight is acceptable, then the scrappy methodology in CPG has severe challenges to overcome.

Approaches That Have Yet to Be Fully Tested

The External Entrepreneurial-Venture Arm

We have now witnessed two companies create similarly unique and interesting scenarios. These were entrepreneurial organizations built to purposefully be outside the corporate mother ship and tasked to ideate, create, and launch new brands and new technologies that the main organization would want, and that they would literally "sell" back into their organization in order to gain their ongoing funding. Each group was envisioned as a reverse M&A (mergers and acquisitions) arm that didn't just *identify* companies for their parent organization to buy, but they had to *create* them from scratch. In one of the two scenarios, the innovation group was even allowed to have their personal incentive plans structured so that *they were compensated* for every sale back into the organization, similar to how entrepreneurs have founders' equity.

For both examples, the teams were freed from the majority of the structure of the main company and allowed to operate as their own organization, building and launching opportunities on their own. This helped to remove the innovation team from being bogged down by all of the internal structural challenges of the large company. With each group seeming to be well-funded, tasked with speed, and given the freedom to operate beyond the internal walls of the large company, the model had the possibility of delivering disruptive innovations in ways considered new and unique for a large Fortune 500 CPG manufacturer.

So what happened to these external entrepreneurial-designed innovation teams? In one situation, a new CEO came into the company six months after the team was formed, redefined their priorities, and tasked them with only doing launches on the internet. While internet launches aren't a bad idea, it's not where the company makes more than 90 percent of its revenue (grocery and convenience stores). At present, a few years since this group's inception, we are waiting to see how this group will translate their direct-to-consumer internet launches into successful on-shelf product lines.

The second situation is new and just developing, but it appears that their initial funding might become a primary limiter. Since they are not tied into the processes of the main organization, they already lack the benefit of the necessary support systems that the mother ship would require from them such as legal, regulatory, operations, and even HR—all which will factor into how many things they can realistically work on. And due to the "urgent" need they have to invent and then sell something back that is worthwhile before they run out of funding, the challenge is going to be having enough money and ideas to make something come out before they lose their runway. We'll keep our eye on this model and see how it progresses in the future.

The Well-Funded and Flexible Entrepreneur

When Jonathan worked as an out-of-the-house entrepreneur for Clorox, he found himself in what seemed to be a very unique and dynamic scenario. He was tasked as a single-person innovation team focused on bringing unique pre-vetted ideas to life—ideas that the company itself desired to go after—with plenty of resources and funding at his fingertips to do what needed to be done. He had access to a cross-functional team—marketing, supply chain, R&D, finance, and legal—inside the company that acted as an amplified support system, both breaking down barriers and linking the projects to the best internal and external resources. This allowed him to accomplish more than a single entrepreneur could ever do on their own.

And aside from regular progress updates, Jonathan was treated like an entrepreneur—and mostly left alone to pursue the *right way* to bring the individual innovation to life, or kill it in its tracks and find something else to focus on. If an internal system within Clorox was slow, too narrowly focused, or less beneficial to the desired needs of the project, Jonathan had the freedom to find a better external system and—more importantly—the funding to go and utilize that resource. If the external systems lacked the sophistication needed to meet the challenge, Jonathan used his Clorox team to fire up the proper internal systems.

Anytime he ran into a barrier, the cross-functional team would figure out ways around it, or define alternate routes. When he approached the team and said, "Hey, I need to get this custom bottle mold made," the team would start making calls to their supplier network, and within two weeks, he could have the mold built in China and be ready to output a new and disruptive bottle structure. With the time, space, and ability to continually edit, adjust, and modify the internal and external approach to a range of new and disruptive ideas, multiple powerful opportunities started to emerge.

With all the freedom in the world to do what needed to be done for a project, along with the flexibility, speed, and endless resources of a big company, it was a beautiful, collaborative, and disruptive environment. Jonathan was able to use his experience at OxiClean to move swiftly on the development and growth of exciting ideas, and he had the support to push, adjust, and modify the concepts with the biggest opportunities in a way that made the most sense for the consumer, the retailer, and the overall business model.

Sadly, the demise of this structure was no more complicated than a shift in leadership at the very top. Within two weeks of a new CEO stating, "We're going to focus our growth on our base brands and existing categories," about four years' worth of work preparing the company to launch into new and adjacent categories simply ended.

* * *

These are just a few of the more common disruptive innovation models that we've seen, but we would be remiss not to mention that there are plenty of large CPG companies that have found an innovation model and approach that they find very successful. Still, we have seen that the more successful groups are focused on line extensions and close-in opportunities, while the disruptive and agile teams tend to struggle. The challenge then is how to create *and sustain* disruptive innovation efforts within these large organizations for more than just a handful of years.

It's a challenging point of tension, but what you can see from the examples above is that innovation teams are continually trying to be just a touch outside of the organization to avoid being bogged down by internal systems and to have the freedom to act more entrepreneurially. But they *need* to also be inside the system to some degree to leverage its funding, resources, and expertise where applicable.

So large CPGs *can* create the kind of disruptive ideas that entrepreneurs are doing far more frequently than large CPG manufacturers. Even if varying political leadership continually creates and then collapses new models of disruptive innovation, that just means they haven't bought into the long-term potential. What, then, is the right way forward?

THE WAY FORWARD

Big companies have amazing teams, talent, depth of knowledge and data, strong existing relationships, and more. There are certainly many challenges—some covered in chapter three—that create limitations in flexibility, but there's nothing stopping you, a large CPG manufacturer, from being a leader of innovation like any other entrepreneurial competitor.

INSIGHT: The goal for innovation teams in large organizations is finding the sweet spot between leveraging the strength of a big company's assets while having the freedom and risk tolerance to operate like an entrepreneur—and then rethinking how you define success.

Regardless of the innovation model your team utilizes, the trick is to **shift how you approach innovation work *and* how you get the organization to accept and believe the results, outlook, and horizon of the most disruptive innovation efforts.** That means creating, testing, and proving your disruptive ideas in such a way that the organization feels confident your ideas are worth the investment and resources.

When you do that, it will require different thinking, because you're going to market in a different way, and that means redefining success. For most of our big clients, if an idea can't produce a $25 million year-one launch, as indicated by BASES, Acupoll, or other concept tests, then it's a no-go.

But what if there was another way to pre-validate your bigger and more disruptive ideas that created a new pathway for realizing them? What if success for a disruptive idea was defined as only $100,000 or $50,000 in revenue, in a smaller footprint that did not tax the organization for the first year? One that created an engaged consumer base, made an impact on its category, and started to capture a new and developing trend and consumer need. In essence, a whole different way to be able to prove that an idea had potential.

QUOTE: *"You can collide [a new product idea] with reality a lot earlier, without it being perfect, without it going into thirty thousand points of distribution in the first year. Because strange things can happen—you can have the best product idea in the world and it doesn't catch on, or you can have the worst idea and everyone could go crazy for it.*

*"If you have an idea that seems really weird, which means it could be really big, then go! Go fast and start **colliding with reality** as soon as you can!*

"And build a culture that it's OK if it doesn't work and you get made fun of. Amazon didn't care if people thought they were doing stupid things... But don't spend a lot of money doing it.

"Think about how [the movie] Field of Dreams cost $5 million to make and was one of the best movies of all time with a great financial return. Waterworld, one of the most expensive movies, was one of the greatest flops in movie history. Be more Field of Dreams. You have to start to talk to real people and collide it with reality before you will totally know what the margins are and whether you can build a sustainable business model around it."

—SHANE EMMETT,
former CEO of Health Warrior, and entrepreneur-in-residence,
Robins School of Business, the University of Richmond

We're suggesting that disruptive ideas inside large organizations can use an entrepreneurial approach to live, grow, adapt, iterate, and protect ideas that become something powerful before being "fully launched." So, we recommend that you:

- Build a culture where failure is allowed, encouraged, and used to learn and improve.

INSIGHT: How does one actually build a culture that allows failure? Well, the people over at Endava have a great pithy article that spells it out in this way: (1) Lead by example—the leaders have to show they can fail too; (2) The importance of following up—when a failure happens, talk about it and make it a teaching moment; (3) Encourage solutions from all level of the organization; (4) Transparency—sometimes failures happen because of limitations: time, resources, and money, and not because the thinking was wrong; (5) Fail fast—try to make an MVP to validate your thinking before going much further, 6) Create simulations—test your thinking over and over; and (7) Eliminate penalties—make the culture blame free.[20]

- Treat disruptive ideas differently and use a wholly separate methodology for testing and proving them to your stakeholders.

---

20 Teodora Cheta, "How to Create a Company Culture that Encourages and Withstands Failure," *Endava* (blog), January 14, 2020, https://www.endava.com/en/blog/Business/2020/How-to-create-a-culture-that-encourages-and-withstands-failure.

- Practice holistic, adaptive iterations—bring the whole idea forward—as fast as possible.

- Recategorize and redefine what success looks like, matching risk and rigor.

- Getting to what consumers **do** in voting with their wallets™ versus what they **say** in testing.

- Outsource the areas or pain points that cause bottlenecks.

QUOTE: *"Mission Field® makes it easy to assess the potential gaps between what consumers say and what they do. There is no substitute for real-world, transactional learning that measures the strength of a total product offering by a consumer's willingness to pay their hard-earned money to own."*

—SCOTT MARCOUX,
Director of Consumer Market Intelligence,
Morning Foods, General Mills

WELCOME TO EMBR

Building upon our decade of helping big CPG companies, the Mission Field® methodology of new product innovation is called EMBR (pronounced "ember"). It's a process that helps you take an entrepreneurial approach to making your disruptive ideas happen. For some, it can get around what may be holding them back, while for others, it can enhance the elements they already have developed internally. It can fit comfortably before, in between, or outside of your existing stage gates. **EMBR is built to help you create, iterate, classify, build, and de-risk your more radical ideas and identify in detail the consumer behavior changes required by them.**

In the end, you'll be able to manage some of your best and most disruptive ideas from beginning to end, and you'll be able to launch platforms of opportunities that the main organization might never have thought were possible, bringing change to the marketplace, new products to consumers, and driving growth for your company.

CHAPTER FIVE

THE EMBR PROCESS

*"Failure is an option here. If things are not failing, you
are not innovating enough."*

—ELON MUSK

The best way to illustrate our solution to *the challenges of large
company innovation*—our EMBR process—is to share some
insights from SpaceX. It may seem odd to use a very large, multibillion-dollar space exploration company to describe the opportunities of large consumer packaged goods innovation, but that's
exactly the point. These are industries that are quite different, yet
the insights and approaches are applicable.

And let's be honest for a moment—SpaceX is doing actual rocket
science. Manufacturing a cookie, or a soda, or an energy bar is

certainly challenging, but not the same thing. Still, if SpaceX can disrupt its category—one currently dominated by trillion-dollar federal governments and NASA's billion-dollar budget—then it provides an analog to where we want large CPG to go, and it gives us a great set of insights into all the lessons we'd like you to learn.

To help illustrate these points, consider the following. Elon Musk recently gave a tour to a passionate YouTube science geek called the Everyday Astronaut, and in that tour, he describes many of the philosophies of EMBR and how we believe it can apply to large consumer packaged goods. In this multi-hour tour, across several videos, Elon describes key elements of the SpaceX innovation process, risk taking, and making choices that apply directly to the opportunities of innovation within consumer packaged goods.[21]

Insight #1: The Importance of Having a Vision and Constantly Pushing the Innovation Envelope. "The rate of innovation is not going to be constant. We have to either increase the rate of innovation or [expect it to naturally] slow down. If you look at America's access to space with an astronaut crew, [NASA] was able to go to the moon in '69, then with the space shuttle we could only go to low earth orbit, then the space shuttle retired and for almost a decade America had no access to space. This is a pretty bad trend, extending to zero. We need a very strong trend in the other direction in order to have any chance whatsoever to make life multiplanetary."

---

21 Everyday Astronaut, "[Summer 2021] Starbase Tour with Elon Musk [Part 1]," August 3, 2021, video, 53:16, https://www.youtube.com/watch?v=t705r8ICkRw; Everyday Astronaut, "[Summer 2021] Starbase Tour with Elon Musk [Part 2]," August 7, 2021, video, 1:10:18, https://www.youtube.com/watch?v=SA8ZBJWo73E.

The key takeaway from this point is to **maintain a bold, powerful vision of what your innovations should seek to accomplish.** By using the analog of how NASA lost its leadership and vision for the space program, Musk also reveals why large organizations need to not only think big, but also put their foot on the gas pedal of innovation in order to keep from returning to a slow and incremental pace of progress.

Insight #2: Pushing the Boundaries. "[SpaceX is] washing our laundry in public. There is always dirty laundry in any program. It's a question of whether it is seen or not. We're intentionally iterating the design rapidly, and with our spaceships and boosters...[we either need to] blow them up, or we have to find a place to store them. And we don't have a lot of space to store them. So we actually want to push the envelope. Plus, if we don't push the envelope we can't achieve the goal of a fully rapid and reusable rocket. We have to go close to the edge [and push our safety] margins."

What's fascinating about this comment is that Elon Musk recognizes that everything SpaceX builds needs to have a purpose. If they are making prototypes, they shouldn't sit on the shelf—they should be used. It's OK if these prototypes fail and spectacularly explode, as long as the company learns something from the experience. Similar to CPG, it's not that large companies need to launch products that will potentially harm consumers, but **it should *always* be the goal to try out new ideas even if they aren't perfect**. If the product doesn't exactly deliver the benefits, or if the packaging has some challenges, then there's an opportunity to learn what is most important to improve upon because maybe it's not the feature that you think is the number one priority that needs a change.

Insight #3: Categorizing Your Innovation Efforts and Scaling Success. "We have a fundamentally different optimization for Starship (a highly experimental heavy-lift reusable rocket designed to go to Mars) versus Dragon (the capsule that holds astronauts). In Dragon there can be no failures, ever. Everything has got to be tested six ways to Sunday. There has to be tons of [safety] margin. There can never be a failure for any reason whatsoever. That's extreme conservatism. Then Falcon (a lighter payload-bearing rocket that can land after takeoff) is a little less conservative. It's possible for us to have a failure of the booster on landing. That's not the end of the world. For Starship...we're iterating rapidly in order to create the first ever fully reusable orbital rocket...reusable in a way that it is like an aircraft."

What you'll notice is that Musk isn't requiring SpaceX to treat each of its efforts the same in their testing, development, and determination of success. The same lens should apply with consumer packaged goods. Innovation programs that are going to have immediate national launches will need maximum optimization that perfects every detail, and renovation efforts of major legacy brands need testing to a high level of sensitivity. But tests of other innovations can and should have higher risk profiles and looser criteria for success. CPG can't keep treating every test of innovation in the same way, as if they were all nationally launched.

We firmly believe that the key insight here is to **categorize the various types of innovation efforts and the levels of risk that they come with, and then set different criteria and evaluation methodologies for each effort that helps to manage that risk.**

Insight #4: Embedding Iteration and Cultural Risk-Reward Asymmetry. "[NASA's Challenger] space shuttle had almost no room for iteration because there were people on board. So you couldn't be blowing up shuttles. A lack of iteration was the problem. A lot of the [safety] issues [that existed] they were already aware of, but people were too afraid to make a change. There was a risk-reward asymmetry. [You were going to get a] big punishment if you make a change and something goes wrong. If you make a change and it goes right, a small reward...Starship does not have anyone on board, so we can keep blowing things up."

While the failures of the *Challenger* space shuttle are a complex story, what Musk is calling out is that the framework of both NASA's culture and the design of the space shuttle created little room for error and high risks for those wishing to make changes or call out problems. Large CPG may be able to see a little of themselves in NASA in that they want to do absolutely no consumer harm such as making someone sick, or having a product that causes a customer problems.

But food and chemical safety is one thing that can be tightly managed—**creating an environment where taking business risks is acceptable is another.** In most large CPGs, business risk taking is not rewarded enough to make it worth someone's career, and that's mostly because the risks of launching an emerging or disruptive opportunity are naturally high due to a system optimized for an all-or-nothing proposition. **If organizations had a way to give themselves more room to iterate and improve upon their initial efforts, then innovations would not have to launch perfectly every time without space for error or improvement.**

Insight #5: Creating Urgency. "The one thing you cannot replace is time. There's a long list of things to solve...so you have to measure the time-risk associated with something."

Every innovation manager knows that there are more things to do in a day than can be accomplished, and the challenge is not just to figure out your priorities and get focused on them, but also to recognize that some opportunities need less testing and proof points to move forward than others. Urgency should be placed on progressing the greatest long-term potential, not the largest short-term ones.

For example, suppose an innovation team is both improving the packaging for a going product and launching a new formula with a new brand in a new category for the company. What we often see is that the packaging change gets more of the attention and that *there is less urgency* to study the more disruptive and financially rewarding opportunity. This behavior is most likely because the new formula or brand offers a higher risk/reward scenario so there is a natural inclination to take the time to flesh out every detail and perfect it. Meanwhile, the packaging change becomes the priority because it impacts a going business and its 1 to 2 percent effect will have financial consequences.

But if you think about it from a "how do I win with innovation" lens, it makes little sense to prioritize the packaging change over the new brand. **The only option that will truly grow the company is to take on the disruptive innovation, and the only way to get the maximum benefit out of your time and risk opportunity costs is to feel comfortable with the risks of moving fast and the imperfectness that comes with speed.**

Insight #6: Working with Ambiguity and Testing Incomplete Completeness. "It's very important to appreciate that everything you see here is a work in progress. What was said last week may be untrue this week. [We often find] we come up with a better idea. [In preparing the rockets to do a test launch] we're going to stack them with a crane because otherwise we'd have to wait for all of the [launch tower] mechanisms to work [which are being built and take time]. We are assembling the launch tower arms and basically putting a mech-zilla together, but in the meantime we could be launching. So let's not wait for the tower to be completed."

The lesson here is that **ideas can and should be tested with any level of completeness in which they exist as a comprehensive unit**. SpaceX is not trying to perfect all the components before they assemble and test their next rocket. They want to test *the whole* of what they have and learn from it without waiting for everything to be dialed in. They are triangulating the insights they gather to make sure that when the final rocket is built, they have seen the cause and effect of multiple components on the rest of the elements. CPG can learn how to do that as well. **The shorthand for this is: test early and often.**

Insight #7: Trying to Perfect That Which Should Not Exist. "The most common error of a smart engineer is to optimize the thing that should not exist...Everyone's been trained in high school and college that you have to answer the question [you're given]. It is convergent logic. You can't tell your professor, 'Your question is dumb,' or you'll get a bad grade. So everyone, without knowing it, has a mental straightjacket on. They will work on optimizing the thing that should simply not exist."

This last point is a powerful one as it suggests that when the train leaves the station, it's normal human behavior to focus on how to improve the little pieces of what you have instead of taking a step back and seeing the whole challenge or problem. Innovations often get launched in this way. The ball gets rolling and each function focuses on delivering their component of the idea. Sometimes **you need to step back, look up, and reevaluate where you're heading** and reconsider the changes that are being made to the platform to determine if it makes sense or if you're straying too far from the core of the insight.

So in summary, the philosophy of EMBR is about:

- The Importance of Having a Vision and Constantly Pushing the Innovation Envelope

- Pushing Boundaries

- Categorizing Your Innovation Efforts and Scaling Success

- Embedding Iteration and Cultural Risk-Reward Asymmetry

- Creating Urgency

- Working with Ambiguity and Testing Incomplete Completeness

- Trying to Perfect That Which Should Not Exist

EMBR: ENERGIZE, MAKE, BURST, ROAR™

ROAR

REGIONAL LAUNCH

Entrepreneurial incubation and launch for distributive ideas and business models

BURST

TRANSACTIONAL TESTING

Sell & learn with prototype product in any channel of distribution (e-comm. to trad. retail)

MAKE

PRODUCT PROTOTYPES

Create and produce sellable prototypes for retail testing

ENERGIZE

STRATEGY, INSIGHTS & CONCEPTS

Creating insights & strategies that develop winning innovation platforms & concepts

The process we call EMBR has four components that shepherd innovative ideas from their genesis (*Energize*), through a rapid stage of entrepreneurial prototype creation (*Make*) and transactional testing (*Burst*), all the way through to a small-scale launch (*Roar*). It's both a process and a toolbox. You can use the elements individually or in sequence. In the coming chapters, we'll dive into each stage of the process in much greater detail. But first, let's look at the overall objectives of the philosophy and why EMBR is so essential.

The EMBR philosophy is fundamentally a comprehensive validation process dedicated to ending all of the various disconnects in CPG innovation processes. EMBR puts depth and breadth together, letting teams take manageable risks for different types of projects and ideas, and utilizing methodologies that permit iteration, improvement, and allow consumers to "show me" based on real-life actions. It's also about rethinking what elements within a large system are holding you back and why, and taking the entrepreneurial approach of not just imagining new ways to make action happen, but making sure innovations will work on their own and can be properly validated before the organization commits its effort to them.

INSIGHT: The EMBR philosophy seeks to iteratively triangulate insights on new innovation opportunities comprehensively in multiple ways to lower risk and build confidence.

First, by making them powerful.

Second, by making them real.

Third, by letting consumers vote with their wallets™.

Fourth, by letting you iterate and pivot all along the way.

When an idea feels risky to an organization, it becomes extremely challenging to go forward with it. That's where EMBR comes in. The EMBR process links the creativity of innovation to the end goal of execution and helps identify if the opportunity is worth the risk. From the very first stages of development all the way through to product launch, this methodology establishes a line of sight from the creative team to the manufacturers, retailers, and consumers. **When we say it is comprehensive and stops the disconnects, we mean that EMBR actually pushes, builds, and reframes innovation as a single life cycle, not as compartmentalized parts of a project.**

QUOTE: *"Consumer behaviors change at a very rapid pace, and it's never been more important for CPG to deliver solutions to their problems in real time. The ability to gain insight quickly across many different elements of the total product offering is extremely valuable to brand teams."*

—SCOTT MARCOUX,
Director of Consumer Market Intelligence, Morning Foods, General Mills

---

CREATING URGENCY AND PUSHING BOUNDARIES

In most qualitative research, the technique used for fuzzy front-end consumer research and idea generation depends on a standard approach of sitting back and listening to consumers articulate their needs, wants, and problems, then getting their reactions to your idea as a possible solution. In the EMBR process, we recommend flipping that on its head and creating a level of entrepreneurial urgency and action.

Any good innovator, researcher, marketer, R&D scientist, or agency person who has done innovation work long enough knows that 80 percent of what you hear is going to be similar to the last project in the same space. It's one thing to have a formal process, but hard-won experience affords us the insight to know when to push the boundaries and drive hard on clarifying consumers' thinking and reactions rather than accepting broad-based commentary at face value. Entrepreneurs don't sit back and listen to consumers discuss their feelings. They evangelize their concept, then assess how large the audience may be for that idea, and adjust from there.

QUOTE: *"Entrepreneurs don't market research their way to an idea. They see a need/want/desire—it may have been their own—and they go figure out a way to meet that need with a new product. In other words, it's their own idea. I created my breastfeeding T-shirt design when I had a baby and couldn't find an existing nursing shirt that worked for me."*

—CARAGH MCLAUGHLIN,
Managing Director, Mission Field®

Put another way, think about what an investigative reporter does. They don't tackle a new topic by passively waiting for insights and information to come to them. They go and actively seek out the people with the knowledge they need to make a story come to life. They warm up their key contacts to get a sense of their story, then they push and probe and contradict previous statements to see how their subject reacts. If a comment is made, they dig deep to try and understand what lies beneath. And they do it all with urgency and purpose.

INSIGHT: How to dig deeper in research like an investigative journalist. We at Mission Field® have learned the following from having former journalists on our staff: (1) Prepare the investigation—identify what you need to "take the story forward" with your research, (2) Design in time to talk—extend your normal consumer sessions to longer than normal, (3) Insert the "end" at the start—get to the heart of the matter quickly versus building up to it, (4) Open up what is being hidden—recognize what people may be hiding or obfuscating and call it out. Ask for answers. And (5) Rethink the moderator's guide—include time for pauses, reflections, silence, and "show me" moments.

COMPREHENSIVE VALIDATION MAKES IT REAL

There are many standard industry approaches to how new innovations get tested and validated. One common methodology is to test something *deeply*, which means leveraging a highly quantitative approach that outputs an answer with statistical confidence. This route is why digital concept tests have become the industry standard, why eye-tracking shelf studies are growing in relevance, and why large CPGs like to test their new items online using A/B splits of direct-to-consumer (DTC) selling to see how it translates consumer interaction into quantifiable directions.

Another approach is to validate a new idea *broadly*, which involves many different types of testing over time to try to build confidence in the entire proposition in order to de-risk a future launch. This can involve combining multiple elements of testing such as conducting focus groups, then a pricing study, then a study on the package redesign, then an in-home usage study, and so on.

Combining these methodologies usually gives large organizations the level of confidence they need to launch something new and innovative, but even then, getting a winner every time is not that straightforward. As we stated earlier, academics believe that between 70 to 95 percent of new products introduced every year fail.[22] Most products, even with the greatest testing efforts—whether deeply or broadly—encounter critical missteps when they launch.

Interestingly, as experts in innovation, we're not immune to experiencing this ourselves. Over the years, we've worked on product innovations that we considered to be well thought out, carefully strategized, and appropriately tested that still stumbled in ways that were unanticipated. These were ideas that both we and our clients wholeheartedly believed in, ideas with a considerable

---

22 Emmer, "95 Percent of New Products Fail."

amount of research insight behind them. We know it's extremely difficult to develop a disruptive concept and somehow shape it to perfectly match a consumer's wants and needs.

So why can't either depth or breadth of testing be the solution to identifying the unforeseen problems and true validation? This is exactly the point. By overindulging in testing, we're simply looking at it all the wrong way.

Our advice is to throw away the assumption that you need to make everything perfect before an idea goes out the door. Endlessly executing quantitative or qualitative testing has its limits—and learning where that line is and whether to "kill or go forward" needs to take precedence over additional testing. Even the best-tested innovations will not be 100 percent perfect, and they can only be improved upon and truly validated when the innovation is exposed to the consumer in its entirety as early as possible, in as real a way as possible. For example: (A) if your R&D can make something close on the bench without knowing how to scale it, that is the perfect MVP. There's no need to "perfect" the large-scale manufacturing of an idea before you even know if it's worth your time and effort. And if the idea is even crazier, and (B) if making that idea come to life requires too much internal process, just go ahead and give consumers existing products that illustrate the components of the R&D brief and use it as stimuli to talk it out. Imagine a crazy innovation of "spreadable milk." Don't have any idea how to make that? Just show consumers a nut butter and a glass of milk. Let them sip on the milk and spread the nut butter on a cracker all while discussing how they could imagine using that experience in a spreadable form.

QUOTE: *"The challenge for GE appliances is breakthrough innovation. We know how to make washers and dryers...but if it's something that's truly unique, making a decision to invest millions of dollars and make hundreds of thousands is tough. [We want to] get ideas from everywhere, build it at a smaller scale, and test it in the marketplace. That makes it a lot easier to scale up."*

—WAYNE DAVIS,
Innovation and Marketing leader, GE Appliances[23]

That is what *comprehensive* validation is about. If the innovation is disruptive, a comprehensive approach thinks about how to build in rounds of iterative enhancements and improvements that constantly test all of its elements together—no matter what stage of development it's in.

Making it real is the second half of the equation. Here's a great way to think through it:

- Do you have a clear vision of the problem you're solving but not the concept? *Identify the best one with a bunch of roughed-out ideas.*

- Do you have a great formula but no unique packaging? *Validate it with basic off-the-shelf six-sided*

23 Jonathan Bacon, "Why Brands Are Abandoning Mass-Produced Products," Marketing Week, October 7, 2015, https://www.marketingweek.com/why-brands-are-abandoning-mass-produced-products/.

packaging—or better yet, grab your competitor's packaging and mock it up to be your brand.

- Are you unsure what brand it should go under? *Check to see which brand works the best by testing it under multiple brands.*

- Do you not have an R&D brief, or even a formula, yet? *Put a competitive product in someone's mouth and describe it in a way that fits your concept.*

- Can you only make fifty prototypes of the idea? *Put it on the shelf and validate it with all the complexities and challenges that selling a live product presents.*

The important thing to realize is that making the product into as close to real-life situations as possible helps us identify key and necessary adjustments that we might not be able to see until it's too late.

QUOTE: *"Most [new products] don't work. That's kind of a given. The trick is to learn from those things that don't work. Prototype something or do a mock-up to get a response from the people you are trying to sell to."*

—GEORGE DERISO,
Professor of Entrepreneurship,University of Colorado

ITERATE ENDLESSLY

So, how does the EMBR process help your innovation efforts? By leveraging an entrepreneurial and iterative approach to the innovation life cycle that looks something like this:

You dream up a new idea that solves a problem. Then, while studying your target audience, you interactively develop and iterate the concept as you go. You don't stand back and just get reactions from people—you push and prod to get to the "yucks and yeahs" that you need to hear.

You build up ideas that create real consumer passion and stave off attempts to water them down. Then you challenge everything that you think is true. You bring in competitive ideas from the category and ideas from different categories that help you bring a key element to life, and then you push for the outer boundaries of what could be—*and you purposefully step too far.* That tells you where the line is so you can bring it back into a more strategic solution.

INSIGHT: How to step a little too far in ideation. The best way to push the boundaries of ideation is to think like a child and be more playful than pure about what your brand stands for. Children have very flexible perspectives on what should and should not be true and are often great at thinking out of bounds. If you are managing a soup brand, a child might say, "Why don't you have crackers because crackers go with soup?" Or perhaps, "Why don't you make drinks, because you make something that is a liquid?" So why not test your soup in a whole wide range of different forms that bring your brand's experiences to life without being stuck to its existing form and shape? It may sound unusual, but that is the whole idea of one step too far. It's quite possible that showing a soup-based beverage is what eventually lands you in the space of a V8 Fusion—a drinkable tomato and vegetable juice. And just imagine if you were the first player in that space today!

However, you're not done yet. You now need to get out of the focus-group room and make it real, so you make a little and sell a little. It's not perfect, but it gets you learning—a lot. You learn what works or doesn't work, and you tweak the idea again. Iterate, return, repeat. Small, fast, iterative.

INSIGHT: Test your products like an entrepreneur would. Make a little and sell a little, learn what worked or didn't work, and tweak the idea. Then you make a little and sell a little more. Iterate, return, repeat, and triangulate your insights into bigger opportunities.

Through this series of product iterations, you not only find out whether the idea worked or didn't work, but you also learn what parts elevate the idea and what is weighing it down. And you learn the reality of the innovation's greatest challenge. From this, you can "triangulate the data" to get to a stronger place. After all, it's one thing to declare that an idea was a failure; it's another thing to be able to say, "The idea didn't work because this element was off, but we know how to make it better," or, "The idea didn't work as well as we'd hoped because the location, pricing, packaging communication, brand perception, etc. was too disconnected from the consumer's desired shopping experience, but we know how to fix it."

Even the most well-thought-out ideas require adjusting and iteration to give them the best chance of success. Indeed, all ideas need tweaking, and they need to be assessed in the real world, in front of real consumers. But it's more than simply testing in the real world. It's about iterating. We can't overemphasize the importance of this, because it's the hook of the whole EMBR process: ***Iteration and adjustment from a real-world testing process are essential.***

INSIGHT: Actions speak louder than words, and that is never more true than when conducting learning experiments to help create, refine, or launch new products. Time and time again we have seen that it is better to observe what consumers and shoppers *do* when given a chance to behave without observation rather than what they might *say* out of the context of their real lives.

There's iteration in the concept stages. There's iteration in the making stages. There's iteration in the testing process. Each and every stage has its own way of incorporating this very critical iterative work.

Through EMBR, we advocate focusing on a *holistic solution* for a *real consumer* from *beginning to end*. Don't fall into the trap of zooming in too closely on the individual pieces of a project. Instead, we recommend maintaining a longer view, keeping an eye on both the shopping experience and the eventual moment that consumers will use the new product in their home.

INSIGHT: Let's stop tearing apart components that are highly interrelated.

Now that we've looked at why things are the way they are, studied and diagnosed the complexity of disruptive innovation challenges, reviewed different ways forward, and shared the overall objectives of the philosophy of why EMBR is essential and powerful, let's look at *what to do* in part two.

How do you begin implementing this holistic EMBR approach? How do you kickstart a new concept in a way that doesn't lose sight of the end goal?

Let's take a look.

NEW WAYS TO DO INNOVATION

CHAPTER SIX

ENTREPRENEURIAL INNOVATION: ENERGIZE

How do you keep the best, most disruptive ideas alive within a system that tends to default to harmonizing, simplifying, and conforming innovations to fit an existing model? How do you nurture ideas in a way that has staying power despite the fact that the validation tools have a way of compressing their opportunity? How do you drive urgency and bring the entrepreneurial spirit into front-end innovation work?

These are great questions to ask when innovators face situations like:

> "I have a powerful brand, but how can I make it address a new consumer target, need, or occasion?"

"How do I best bring to life a new technology or product that R&D has created?"

"How do I know if an idea we're working on is going to turn into a successful, breakthrough launch?"

Our answer to these questions is *Energize*, the first stage of the EMBR methodology. *Energize* is a model of iterative, design-focused creation guided by deeper, more meaningful, and realistic consumer feedback with a pushing and probing research model. Through Energize, you can accomplish a series of benefits like training your gut, gaining insights, and matching rigor to risk. You finish the up-front work of innovation creation with platforms, concepts, R&D direction, and visual graphics that *holistically* bring the idea to life in line with your strategic goals. Simply put, you take a lot of swings at the plate and uncover the right ones that should be carried forward. You are probably already practicing some of the strategies discussed in this chapter, but the *Energize* model should give you a few surprising twists and new perspectives to challenge existing norms.

Think of this as our desire to share how we've adapted various innovation models to overcome different clients' challenges over Mission Field®'s ten-year history of leading innovation efforts. Over time it's important to continually refine your own methodologies as you will have gained important lessons and insights along the way.

The best way to bring *Energize* to life is by addressing six aspects of the early stages of innovation development:

1. Understanding the Guardrails

2. Generating Powerful Ideas with Six Points of Ideation

3. Recruiting the Right Consumers

4. Bringing Ideas to Life

5. Pushing to the Wall of the Outer Boundaries

6. Iterating Dynamically

1. UNDERSTANDING THE GUARDRAILS

When kicking off a front-end innovation project, it's not unusual to find that the project team is always very clear on the strategy, opportunity, risks, and rewards of what they want to accomplish. They know the business reason for why they need to uncover new ideas, the target audience that they want to serve, and the general direction they think they need to go—and they provide us with copious amounts of information that bring those points to life.

But we have also found that behind those clear and compelling business objectives is a series of stakeholders who have their own assumptions, concerns, fears, curiosities, experiences, unstated beliefs, and perceptions that all need to be uncovered around how, why, and whether the organization will be able to pursue a specific innovation path.

We can all agree that organizational stakeholders need to be involved in shepherding new innovation efforts and should be engaged in, if not championing, the process. But our main point is about extracting the mental mapping of both the expected output and the organization's, and possibly even the retailer's, perceived boundaries of the opportunities (**in other words, "what needs to be true" for a new innovation to be accepted**). Once the concerns, cautions, and frameworks of key stakeholders are mapped out, then it's easier for the innovation team to understand how to map what the consumer wants against the guardrails of the company and the retailer. Often in innovation, those two things are in conflict before the process of idea generation even gets started.

> **INSIGHT: Retailer Interviews.** There are many examples where we embed discussions with retail buyers and category managers into a front-end innovation project because the guardrails that they illuminate need to be addressed in the research project. This can be as simple as clarifying margin hurdles, shopper behavior, or even the prioritization of where the retailer wants to see their category go in the future.

As an example, we recently engaged a brand that had not innovated on its main line in several decades. They knew the lack of innovation was hurting their brand, and they had to do something significant or risk continuing to suffer a long and slow downward spiral that had been underway for years. The project team outlined the myriad of innovation opportunities and challenges the organization had faced over the decades—and it didn't look good.

This company had multiple decks of well-thought-through innovation ideas, many rounds of concept testing on similar ideas, and a substantial number of strategic decks outlining the issues. Years into the effort they had little to show for it except continuing downward trends in their category and brand. Yet, with a new management team in place, there was an eager attitude to make something happen. So why were they stuck, and how were they going to fix it?

For this team, the internal *unstated* guardrails were one of the most critical components of being able to progress with their innovation desires. While each department head was hungry to make a change and willing to go after new spaces and new technologies, there were multiple challenges that held them back from being able to *validate* any type of innovation. We saw this expressed both in how they viewed ideas that had been launched in the past and how they were likely to view any new ideas in the future.

One of the simplest examples was margins. There was no single, agreed-upon financial structure by which a new innovation would be measured. Some leaders felt that a successful new innovation had to deliver margins equal to its existing product line, one that ran at high efficiency behind decades of manufacturing expertise, or it would not be worth the effort. Others felt that a "legacy" level of expectation was unrealistic and needed to be reframed for the costs of working with co-manufacturers, new technology, and even new channels of distribution. Without a specific agreed-upon metric and approach, innovation efforts were going to be stalled if this topic was not integrated early on into the process of idea evaluation and determining success.

2. GENERATING POWERFUL IDEAS WITH SIX POINTS OF IDEATION

While we could write another entire book on the methodology of new product idea generation, we have found that one of the simplest ways to come up with good ideas is to push your team's thinking beyond their current frameworks.

To that end, we love this six points of ideation model for idea generation:

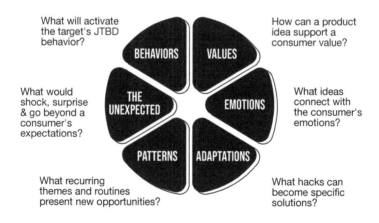

Behaviors—What will activate the target's job to be done (JTBD) behavior?

Or, stated a different way, what jobs are consumers hiring the new product to do for them? This is one of those straightforward elements that innovation teams are often thinking about. They have a strategy in mind such as "make our brand relevant in a new category," and the goal everyone is tasked with is to develop a new product idea that activates a consumer behavior.

How do you make this happen? It's not as simple as coming up with a good idea that consumers want. You have to go deeper into understanding who they are and what causes them to take action today. This can be done as easily in time-pressed focus groups as in ethnography work. **The key is knowing how and where to dig and what to listen for as they describe their own points of activation.** Remember that JTBD focuses on the "why" behind the consumer behavior, and as it was famously said, "People don't want to buy a quarter-inch drill. They want a quarter-inch hole."

Values—How can a product idea support a specific consumer value?

Consumers all come with a set of beliefs about the world and their movement within it. It's the innovator's task to clarify the nuances between the bold and broad statements they'll provide you with in research to get at a more fundamental truth about their value system. We've done enough research on food products to know that "health" is a flexible and fungible value statement—a continuum of truth where foods fall on a scale of "more or less healthy."

A mom who approves of their kids eating their favorite marshmallow cereal can describe its relative healthfulness in real and honest terms (e.g., "It's much better than letting them have a candy bar. Healthiness is having them eat something over nothing. Sometimes that's all we have in the house. They are healthy when they are happy."), and so can a mom who only allows their kids to eat organic granola (e.g., "I want to see real ingredients in their breakfast. I think sugary cereals are bad for growing bodies. I like that some granola has chocolate chunks since that gets them to eat healthy.").

Both products can bring roughly the same amount of sugar, carbs, fat, and whatever else you want to point out within the eating occasion, they just do it in different ways. **The key is to peel back the onion on the values that people carry with them and see how it informs their choices so you can build ideas that serve the needs of your target best.**

Emotions—What ideas connect with the consumer's emotions?

Closely related to values is the consumer's emotional link to things connected to the opportunity space. This includes things like the *occasion* (e.g., the midmorning pick-me-up), the *ingredients* (e.g., the warming effect of cinnamon), or even the *brand* itself (e.g., the nostalgia of a specific product line). They can all connect with the consumer on an emotional level. **The key is to listen for those times when emotions pop out and inform the innovation opportunity, then build on or heighten those emotional aspects.**

Adaptations—What hacks or workarounds can be turned into a specific solution?

One of our favorite pathways to innovation brainstorming and creation is to watch people customize, hack, or adapt something they already use. We all do it when cooking a meal. You may add more of this or less of that to make it exactly what you want. To watch consumers do this same process with a branded item is always fascinating. **The key is to look beyond the specifics of the hacks to the intentionality of what they were trying to accomplish to inform new thinking.**

Patterns—What recurring themes and routines present new opportunities?

We are all creatures of habit, and the way we return to products and engage with them speaks volumes. Those patterns indicate what feels comfortable and easy to adopt for your target audience. Does your target happen to control the size of their sweet treat after a meal by breaking their current cookies in half? Maybe your next cookie innovation needs to adapt to their patterns by offering cookie halves, bites, or muffin tops. **The key is to look for patterns within the systems that make sense for your target and build or solve for those needs.**

The Unexpected—What would shock, surprise, and go beyond a consumer's expectations?

Sometimes a surprisingly ripe target for new product solutions comes from deeply investigating what would surprise, delight, shock, or go beyond the consumer's expectations. For example, we have developed strong, winning ideas by taking a brand's legacy and building it out a step or two. We worked on a traditionally kid-focused product where we took the brand to an adult space by adding adult flavor notes to the expansion. The adults resonated with their nostalgic brand suddenly filling a new space for them and were delighted.

The key is to push the boundaries to find those spaces that get a big reaction, then build on it or scale it back to the sweet spot as appropriate. This mind-blowing space can be a powerful, new place to play.

QUOTE: *"Our consumer validation process is often reactive, working backward to prove consumer need. We need to establish a consumer-first approach to innovation with a proactive learning plan."*

—FORTUNE 500 CPG MARKETING VP

---

3. RECRUITING THE RIGHT CONSUMERS

There are plenty of existing books about consumer research and front-end innovation. For the most part, they contain truisms that we agree with: you need to have empathy for your consumer, you need to listen to what they want, you need to find unmet needs and opportunities, and you need to understand the *job to be done* (JTBD) for the product. But many of the existing books fail to look at product research through the lens of how you recruit consumers and what type of consumers are best adapted for helping you validate the right opportunity.

We've had an opportunity to study the academic research behind consumer testing (not theoretical studies but the practical applicability studies that use real-life behavioral psychology), and the overwhelming consensus of some of the top business professors in the nation is that the *effort* of front-end consumer product testing, in a classic focus-group setting, is flawed. With many years of experience in the CPG field, we tend to look at academic opinions as offering up insights into a theoretical framework. While they're exploring the theory of consumer research, we're living and breathing the application of both research design and execution. So after studying their insights more deeply, we recognized the value of their key insight—the effort of consumer research focused on innovation is often flawed, and it's not because the testing model itself is unsound.

Consumer research on innovation is often flawed because the participant *selection* process is flawed.

Here's why:

The average consumer doesn't always have the type of thinking style that lends itself to analyzing the motivations behind their own behavior or thought patterns. Some people are expressive— they're very good at saying what they think, but they struggle to describe *how* they arrived at their opinions. Others are analytical and cautious—they think carefully through problems but overanalyze every step of their own behavior.

QUOTE: *"There are limits on the degree of 'discontinuousness' that consumers feel comfortable with...and it can be difficult to gain meaningful input [from average consumers]—especially early on in the development process."*

—ROBERT W. VERZYER (1998)[24]

Simplifying the various academic conclusions: most people struggle to look at innovation and understand *how much* it could improve their lives or solve a problem. They have difficulty weighing the loss of a product they currently use against the potential benefits that a future product could bring, and the researchers and marketers asking the questions often thoroughly examine topics that they just haven't examined deeply before.

It's all a question of impact. Think about it for yourself. How would you calculate and then express the relative loss to your life if your car (or cars) disappeared for a month? It should be easy to gauge the impact of your behavior switch to public transportation, the effort of walking everywhere, or the cost of renting a temporary car. But what if I took away your bags of frozen peas for a month? What is the real impact on your life? Would you be happy to just buy frozen corn? Can you quickly express your behaviors? How many consumers have you talked to that can bring this relative loss to life?

---

24 Robert W. Veryzer, "Key Factors Affecting Customer Evaluation of Discontinuous New Products," *The Journal of Product Innovation Management* 15, no. 2 (1998), https://www.sciencedirect.com/science/article/abs/pii/S0737678297000751.

However, there is a type of consumer that exists in all cohorts and demographics but is also harder to spot: individuals with a specific kind of thinking process that allows them to understand and articulate the difference between the loss of what they have today and what they could gain with something new. It's not too hard to find people who can express *why* they are or aren't interested in a product, but it is hard to find self-aware people who can explain their gains and losses, their changes of behaviors, and their overall motivations with enough clarity and detail to help steer our innovations.

> **QUOTE:** *"Radical innovations are very different from the product stored in memories...because they allow consumers to do things they were unable to do before (Hoeffler 2003). As a result...learning costs pose the greatest challenge.* **Consumers may find it especially difficult to access the relevant product category schema for radical innovations** *(Moreau 2001). When they feel that the innovation does not fit the existing schema, they are unsure what knowledge from these schemas can be transferred to the new products (Rindova 2007)....And* **therefore they feel they lack the ability to make effective use of the radical innovation.***"*
>
> —RUTH MUGGE AND DARREN DAHL,
> "Seeking the Ideal Level of Design Newness: Consumer Response to Radical and Incremental Product Design"[25]

25 Ruth Mugge and Darren W. Dahl, "Seeking the Ideal Level of Design Newness: Consumer Response to Radial and Incremental Product Design," *Journal of Product Innovation Management* 30, no. S1 (2013), https://doi.org/10.1111/jpim.12062, emphasis added.

Therefore, the key is to ensure you talk to the right subset of your desired target that not only gives you the most representative responses on new ideas, but also gives responses that can meaningfully guide and build on those ideas. Finding this subset of any demographic group yields participants who are better at evaluating the *importance and impact* of innovation.

At Mission Field®, we've created a proprietary recruiting methodology to find this exact type of consumer—a group we call *Emergent Consumers*. We believe this type of consumer's thinking helps get to bigger ideas faster. Emergent Consumers are naturally able to envision a future state and can *describe* their own feelings about switching away from a product they already know and love to something new and interesting, yet unproven.

The benefits of rethinking who you are talking to—such as using Emergent Consumers in research—is that you can strive to get more in-depth and precise responses. Typical focus-group consumers sometimes report that they are interested in a product, but the underlying reasons for their interest don't match what the product idea intended. But by rethinking who you're talking to, you will be better able to identify false positives (i.e., people who like an idea but for the wrong reasons). With a better recruiting method, you can also identify groups of people who like the idea for the right reasons and can articulate those reasons well. The method we have landed on with recruiting Emergent Consumers we feel helps us fine-tune the opportunity and give us a better context for the continued development of any idea, especially the most disruptive ones.

Emergent Consumers can also help achieve an even deeper level of insight. By testing their reactions to our "inner guardrail" and "outer guardrail" ideas, we can learn what they are ready for and why, and we can articulate the benefits of boundary-pushing ideas to shape strategy and pipelines. We use these insights to develop a vision of where things are headed.

4. BRINGING IDEAS TO LIFE

Making Ideas Real: MVP Thinking

The philosophy of our company, which is steeped in an entrepreneurial mindset, is to make things as *real* as possible as fast as possible, and it's another important key to disruptive ideation. You don't have to make your innovation perfect, you just need an MVP (Minimal Viable Product) to be able to test its possibilities.

QUOTE: *"An MVP is the version of a new product that allows the team to gather the maximum amount of proven customer knowledge with the least amount of effort...to determine further iterations to enhance the value development."*

—ERIC RIES,
Founder, Lean Startup methodology

In many organizations, food or product development comes only after several rounds of testing. Ideas are initially experienced as a couple of lines of text on a page and bounced off of consumers in the hopes of gaining insight based on a description that will inform the R&D or product development. We have found, and believe, that consumers need to *hold* a product—they need to lift it, smell it, taste it, or swirl it around. If a consumer can't get their hands on an idea, you're asking them to do a lot of guesswork in the hopes that their imagination will be helpful.

What if you simply don't have the physical product that you want to test? Let's suppose the idea is for a new cheesy snack product. R&D has an early prototype, but after testing it with a few consumers, you learn that people love the taste but hate the texture. The snack needs to be *a lot* crunchier to have any chance of success, but according to R&D, it will take a lot of time, effort, and money, or they don't have the resources to build Cheesy Snack 2.0. What can you do?

The best way is to build an MVP: a mock-up or proxy of the product. First, don't worry about getting the prototype perfect—the goal is to get close to reality, but anything tangible is closer to reality than words on a page. Second, we believe you can always find existing products that are akin to the idea that you're testing and get some feedback over nothing. Search the universe for anything close to your idea, even if that means looking far afield— to Europe, Asia, or South America. Or just locate multiple products on the market that each have one element of what you want to bring to life, then hand it all to a consumer as a range and say, "If our idea was a little bit like Product A and a little bit like Product B, how would you make it better?" In the case of Cheesy Snack 2.0, you might ask your test group, "What if it had the cheesy flavor of *this* snack, but the crunchy texture of *that* snack, with *this* packaging?"

Some of the products you'll find will be good and some bad, but by putting them in people's hands or mouths and starting a dialogue about what works and why, you will progress your idea more rapidly, and *holistically,* to learn about problems to solve or opportunities to pursue. And you will discover competitive differentiation points or even, with a bit of luck, the root insight of the job to be done.

You can find out *why* people might be interested in Cheesy Snack 2.0. Perhaps they're interested in it as a source of on-the-go fuel between meals, or as an indulgent late-night treat. Or perhaps you discover a deeper insight—the taste reminds consumers of some cheesy treat from the '80s and takes them back to their childhoods. Maybe you discover that consumers want an *engaging* snack, like Oreos, that can be eaten many different ways. These findings inevitably inform how you develop the R&D brief and move the innovation forward.

Invariably, people respond better to something tangible than they do to conceptual ideas on a page. When you allow people to play with competitive products or your MVP, you can learn from moments of delight, moments of frustration,

or consumer experiences that your brand couldn't have reached until much later in the innovation life cycle.

Integrating holistic elements with nascent ideas requires nothing more than creativity, exploration, curiosity, and a healthy dose of strategic vision.

Simple and Appealing Packaging

Another key to bringing ideas to life in *Energize* is being mindful of the physical packaging and what you can realistically say on the package. Keeping in mind the goal of holistic learning, it's important to understand how your brand is going to appear on the shelf and how it's going to communicate what it is and why shoppers might want it. Many concepts on page-based research depend on far too many words to convey what can actually be said on the front of a package. It's easy to forget that in the end you have to deal with the relatively small real estate of a front-of-pack label.

QUOTE: *"Concept testing has its challenges...it's easy to over communicate the offer and never show ideas in context. This can make for an unrealistic test of consumer behavior. It has its purpose, but you can't over rely on it to tell you the truth."*

—JON OVERLIE,
Innovation iSquad Manager, General Mills

If there is no actual packaging to test, you can once again resort to entrepreneurial or guerrilla tactics. Create a design using any means available—cobbling together photos off the internet or "Frankensteining" a homemade model. After adding your logos and branding, mock up a package with an image that approximates how the product might appear in the retail environment. Again, perfection isn't important. It's amazing what you can bring to life with a laser printer, the internet, and an image capture tool, with no design experience necessary.

Words on the package that promise a wonderful experience are worthless if the look is off. After so much effort to create a breakthrough product, you don't want the project to be brought to a screeching halt by consumers who say, "It doesn't look tasty." Remember, we eat with our eyes, so if the product is a food or beverage, the images should look delicious and be prominent. Even if the item is a cleaning product or a nutraceutical, the design elements that provide context and frame your product are critical. One photographed pour of a bathroom cleaner might make it look gentle while another image might make it look powerful—and the one you want depends on the benefits you are trying to convey.

Though this insight may seem elementary, it isn't theoretical and shouldn't be overlooked. We have worked on dozens of products where the internal process—usually based on the products being shown oversized in a PowerPoint deck and in isolation—has relegated the hero imagery behind the branding, name, design, or claims. It doesn't tend to go well, so it's better to learn and correct for it early.

CASE: We recently worked on a project where prior research showed strong signals for success. We were leading a round of focus groups to help move the idea forward holistically. We quickly made packaging mock-ups of the 2D images that existed and put them on a mock competitive shelf. In a "shopping" exercise, the target consumer didn't see the packaging when surrounded by the competition. Once consumers were handed the package, they loved it, but this signaled that something about the design wasn't disruptive enough in the context of the competition. It risked facing challenges at launch. The biggest issue was that the design aesthetics and size of branding overtook the package, and consumers missed the main point of the concept because they didn't know what it was. On top of that, the food image didn't look tasty. The packaging went back for revisions and will certainly adjust with these learnings: big, tasty food imagery with clear claims that help the shopper know "what is it" and "why is it for me."

Branding communication can easily become overcomplicated. Front-end innovation teams occasionally stumble by over-thinking what they're trying to communicate. Either the idea becomes too complicated, or the promises too complex. If you can't boil down an idea to its essence with a couple of sentences, you may be overthinking it or adding too many components to the concept.

It's important in any early stage, as you're designing and creating mock-ups, to *keep it simple*. Create a package that conveys the key concept and looks enticing. When you put the package in front of consumers, take note of reactions such as "I like the words, but I don't like the image," or "I want to know more about X." Then, of course, keep iterating.

QUOTE: *"This is not unlike thinking about who your target audience is. Remember, you can't be all things to all people, so your messaging shouldn't try to communicate all the things to all the people. Ask yourself, 'Why would my target consumer use this?' The answer to that question is what should be in those couple of sentences and on the front of the pack."*

—CARAGH MCLAUGHLIN,
Managing Director, Mission Field®

The important part here is that you are moving the idea forward holistically. When you pull all of the elements together with simple packaging that clearly communicates the brand, the food/product, and the benefits or promises, you can triangulate the consumer's true desire for the idea. That's when an idea can push beyond the original boundaries of what was thought to be possible.

5. PUSHING TO THE WALL OF THE OUTER BOUNDARIES

The *Energize* system identifies possibilities built on a backbone of reality—you imagine only what you can realistically create. This is something we covered a bit earlier when we discussed understanding the company's guardrails. But the consumer has guardrails too. They also have different boundaries for what they would consider realistic and appropriate territories for their favorite brands. To ensure that disruptive, nascent, or cutting-edge ideas receive support, the next step is to find those consumer-driven boundaries, and push up to them and past them with your thinking.

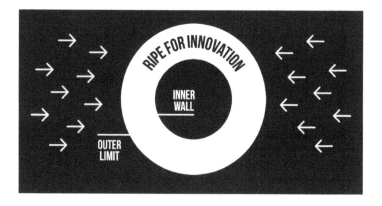

Let's define the boundaries of what consumers feel is not compelling as the "outer wall" of your brand—the parameters of what's not acceptable based on what has been already done and what they know about you. For Cheez-It crackers, this may be the idea of launching a gourmet cheese with no cracker to be found. The "inner wall," as we'll call it, is what makes the most sense to execute *today* while also providing a little bit of incrementality to the core product lines.

Ideas closer to the inner wall most likely use existing technology, existing manufacturing, and are easy for the company to produce. An idea close to the inner wall shouldn't raise too many eyebrows—such as when Cheez-It launched Duos, a mash up of two exciting flavors and textures in the same box.

The "outer wall" is both the outer limit, a space in which an idea will seem too crazy, as well as a place of high incrementality—territories where there's likely little to no crossover with primary products in the main brand. The way to find that outer wall is to propose multiple ideas that fully push on the brand's existing boundaries, then back them up a step, and maybe another step. It's far better to take an absolutely "out there" idea and make it slightly more reasonable until you get consumers' heads nodding than it is to *only* test ideas that are a step or two away from where you are today.

Once you've established these two walls, you know the area that is ripe for innovation—that space will be your playground. You know the risk tolerance of the consumer, and you're much more likely to have the right range of ideas between the safe, easy options and ideas that lead to larger possibilities and a pipeline that can eventually push the brand into new places.

In our experience, many ideas die because they are either too safe or too far out, both for the consumer and for the innovation team. Ideas that are too cautious sometimes come from incredibly smart, experienced people who have been at their companies for years. They know their business objectives, and they're good at generating ideas, but they can't see their own guardrails. They come up with ideas in-house using what they know today, but the ideas they create are framed by what they imagine they *can't* do. Consequently, they avoid spaces that feel unsafe or scary, which can be limiting.

We also see clients hire outside innovators or solicit internal ideation in a way that pushes the boundaries *too* dramatically and produces unrealistic opportunities. Often, these teams were asked to come up with disruptive ideas, but when they did, they realized that their innovation undermined the existing brand or category. So, the company was disincentivized from launching the idea.

CASE: Ten years ago, a well-known cleaning products company came up with a radical innovation that made cleaning much easier and, at the same time, made undercabinet storage far simpler. This invention did amazing things, and when brought to life, it was truly disruptive. The brand's target audience was all-in on the new idea. However, instead of launching the product, the company took a step back and analyzed the situation. They realized that the innovation was going to upend the cleaning products industry, including their own business, so the idea was shelved.

While the innovation surely would have upset the industry and potentially undermined their own products, our message to that company then was perhaps counterintuitive: "Yes, this idea will rock some boats, including your own, but it's better to disrupt yourself than to let someone else do it for you. If a rival company launches the same idea, your company could theoretically be forced to license the rival's technology in order to participate in the revolutionized category." That company needed a series of steps to get them there. This idea was too much, too fast. It just felt too risky. It could have been more palatable if there were smaller steps that helped to extend their thinking and get them to be that ultimate "category converter."

"What if we invented a soda for cats?"

This was an actual idea that popped up in a brainstorming session a few years back. It was crazy. It was bizarre. Every time we tell the story, people chuckle. But even though this idea was beyond the outer guardrail of the consumer's comfort zone, it was a great suggestion because, when we reeled in our thinking one step, we came up with an amazing breakthrough. That product breakthrough—one step back from a cat soda—was based on real human/pet relationship insights, and it's one of the highest-performing ideas we've ever tested.

If you can honor the inside guardrails of a company while simultaneously pushing the outer boundary, you will discover a fun and fascinating playground in between. *Energize* develops ideas that fall inside that range. In doing so, it helps us learn exactly how far consumers will allow a brand to evolve, and it expands the horizon of what a product, brand, or even a category could be.

6. ITERATING DYNAMICALLY

Once you find the area of your playing field, keep all the best ideas rolling and adapting through rounds of iteration, which, as you're probably starting to notice, is a constant drumbeat in our thinking and actions. It's these continual iterations that keep an innovation from stagnating and help you get to new and revolutionary places.

When you receive an underwhelming response from a group of consumers, tweak the idea with new iterations. That's obvious, but what isn't always obvious is that iterations are often called for even when consumers find a product interesting or exciting. Even *positive* feedback doesn't signal the end of iteration.

A few years back, we helped develop a line of pet food treats for a client. We started consumer testing in California and learned that there was a strong demand for fish-based flavors, notably salmon. Consumers were sending us the message that they wanted healthy products for their pets, so we listened. We gathered feedback, and it helped us rank our ideas.

We felt like we had a pretty good handle on what consumers were looking for. However, when we took the same slate of ideas to Boston, consumers were largely disappointed. It turned out, California flavor rankings were largely useless in New England, where the salmon idea was unpopular. As we learned, in the pet-care sector, consumers are inclined to feed their pets the types of foods that they themselves enjoy. This means that a successful iteration of a product in one region may very well fail in another region. Iteration has to continue, even after positive feedback.

Iterative triangulation is important in the *Energize* process. Study the nuances of different sub-target audiences and differences in taste based on geography, taking into account the preferences of men versus women, older consumers versus younger consumers, households with children versus adult-only households, and so on—as appropriate to your target audience subgroup. Each data point from these nuances can guide your development process as you continually iterate a budding idea.

And you don't just have to take our word for it. The concepts we have been testing for clients are coming back with significantly high ratings project after project. For one client across multiple *Energize* projects, 50 percent of our concepts get ranked as "BASES Superstars," 33 percent get ranked as "Brand Builders," and the rest fall into a mix of "Targeted Plays" and other rankings.

The *Energize* process offers an approach to innovation that greatly increases an idea's chance of success. It can help you incorporate all the best insights from the EMBR *philosophies* of how we believe large CPG companies can get to bigger ideas faster while de-risking the process: have a bold vision, push boundaries, balance risk with reward, iterate, allow for failures, drive urgency, be holistic, and step back and review as you progress.

Now, once the *Energize* process shepherds great ideas through development, it's time to *Make.*

CHAPTER SEVEN

SMALL-SCALE PRODUCTION FOR TESTING: MAKE

No good idea should die on a PowerPoint slide. And we're convinced that no good idea *has* to die if you make a little, sell a little, and repeat until you get it right for the consumer, the shopper, the retailer, and your business.

In the CPG world, we're all entrepreneurs at heart. CPG companies are absolutely *full* of people who have amazing ideas that they'd love to turn into reality, but getting an idea produced can be a daunting challenge. True entrepreneurs and innovators are *made* only when they *make* something. We believe ideas are of little value in and of themselves if you can't actually sell them. It's the execution of those ideas that turns debatable hypotheses and theories into hard, cold facts.

QUOTE: *"HighKey often debates should we enter a new category? After R&D comes up with an amazing formula, we incubate it and give it a shot. It's not a profound decision...We don't get too intellectually pure. In my old world [General Mills], we probably would have killed many of our company's launches because they would have been strategically unpure."*

—JOE ENS,
CEO, HighKey

While it might seem like it should be easier for large corporations—who have the power, resources, and manufacturing facilities that entrepreneurs envy—to manufacture a new product, it's often *more* difficult. We've previously discussed how the embedded structure and challenges of large CPG limits its ability to properly assess and value a new innovation. One major barrier we've covered is that the path to production is complex, expensive, and built for scale. The reason why the ability to make a small amount of product is so important is that it is much harder to build confidence and validate the "size of the prize" of a new idea if you aren't able to make enough sellable products to test the business model.

In *Energize*, much of the battle was learning to look for, poke at, and reframe your innovation opportunities. But in the *Make* process, we want to share how large CPG companies can overcome the existing limits of their systems, production equipment, specialized resources, and risk mitigation approaches in order to bring their new ideas to a short and testable life span. We believe that the pathway to making small runs of a new and disruptive product can fit within the system that exists today. Making test batches of new ideas *can* serve the purpose of small-scale testing and validation.

The best way to illustrate these possibilities is to start by looking at five key factors:

1. Beyond the List

2. Reframing the Risk

3. Scale or Bail

4. To Go Big, Think Small

5. Scaling Up the Entrepreneurial Model

1. BEYOND THE LIST

Big CPG companies are incredibly skilled at both benchtop work and scaled production, but executing the step in between— producing a thousand units of sellable product for consumer and real-world testing—can be about as complex as making a million units. The structure simply isn't built for small-scale manufacturing, so making a small run of an innovative product that could help power a test, learn about, and de-risk the idea is akin to asking for a national launch.

QUOTE: *"[In order to make some product] to get an additional bit of in-market learning, it takes about as many resources as the company would normally put into a national launch."*

—FORTUNE 500 CPG MANAGER, Global Innovation Supply Chain

But R&D and production limitations aren't a matter of willpower, philosophical approach, or a need to shift the organization's mindset. On the contrary, most of the obstacles to small-scale production are quite real. It's perfectly understandable why company stakeholders tend to bring forward only the ideas that they know can be executed within the limitations of their preexisting equipment and operational systems.

This is why you need to think like an entrepreneur. Externalize the pain points where the system is correctly limiting your ability to make a little to help progress your learning plan and de-risk a future large-scale launch. The pain point in this case is that the list of available and approved manufacturing options is short, costly, and difficult to utilize. **The way over the wall is to *go beyond the lists* of current production options by finding smaller, more nimble co-manufacturers who know how to get products off the ground and have flexibility born from supporting entrepreneurs.** This is the *Make* process.

In the last fifteen years, we've seen an incredible rise and improvement in the quality of small manufacturing operations that excel at making products at low volumes. These smaller producers could never meet a large company's capacity for mass production or pricing, but they're quite good at creating new products in creative ways. So, when we approach them with a proposition that's not about cranking out high volumes of units, but creating something new, they're highly receptive.

Most smaller manufacturers get genuinely excited about helping create new ideas for a large CPG company. Sometimes, they want to exhibit their value. Other times, they just want to see if they can do it. We always pay them for their time and expertise, and since smaller manufacturers aren't always operating on a packed schedule, they have room for us on their production calendar. It's a win-win.

So why aren't these smaller manufacturers already being utilized? Interestingly, most large CPGs have put into place processes that almost completely prevent them from working with these small co-manufacturers. The way that they validate and approve of a new factory can take years of analysis and hard work before being certified for use. One way that we have helped our clients get around this is to utilize a third-party organization that can act like a speedboat and zip toward a new opportunity, while the main battleship of the organization stays on its steady course without being distracted from its ultimate destination. How, you may ask? By outsourcing the risk to a third-party company (e.g., ourselves) that is able to take on all the risks of production quality, safety, and speed.

QUOTE: *"Anything small and nimble is hard for us to do. Without Mission Field®, this idea never would have gotten off the ground."*

—VP OF MARKETING

So, if you are an innovation leader in a large organization, it shouldn't matter if it feels like you can't readily produce a new item on a limited scale internally, if you can't afford to stop production on existing lines to make way for small-batch manufacturing of a new product, or if you have long start-up times and requirements to bring on a new co-manufacturer. Our solution is simple: *don't stop*. Just keep doing what you do best and think about how you can externalize a path to nimble smaller-scale production.

2. REFRAMING THE RISK

Having access to small-scale production is one thing, but safety and quality controls are also fundamental concerns to all large CPG companies. Everyone we work with strives to ensure that no matter the output, there's zero risk of harm. Everyone is dedicated to protecting consumers, so as part of this attention to safety and quality, CPG companies rigorously qualify all of their co-manufacturers. We love that, but unfortunately, we've seen that within our larger clients, it can often take quite a long time—*nine to twenty-four months*—to qualify a manufacturing facility.

No matter the role of the co-manufacturer, the process is the same. The co-manufacturer might be a food supplier of puffed grains of rice, a facility that has made the same type of cracker for decades, a honey supplier adding a small amount of honey to a formula, or a packaging group making aqueous-proof cartons. It's still the same process, and it can still take up to two years.

We've seen an internal team at a large company identify a co-manufacturer who had been making the same thing for *thirty years*.

The innovation team wanted to use that co-manufacturer's technology to produce a cool new idea, but the organization's need to qualify the producer *their way* put the project on pause for years, even though the co-manufacturer was actively selling products for other brands.

CPG companies need to be consistent. There's no denying that quality is of paramount importance, but those internal protections that serve the consumer when making mass-scaled products don't serve the effort of making new and innovative ideas come to life. The solution is to *reframe the risk*.

To show how the risk can be reframed, we had an interesting scenario where a client wanted to test our approach against their internal approach. They saw it as a head-to-head test in which two innovation teams were vying to compete on speed-to-market of a new idea.

One innovation team handed the risk of the entire process to us, allowing us to qualify multiple co-manufacturers, own the risk of production, and get the product into a small-scale test. By doing that, we made both the effort and the risk *external* to their organization. Meanwhile, another innovation team took the organization's "official" route to qualification and production then adapted a new system *internally,* including changing the organization's process procedures and trying to make the company speed up its overall approach.

While the internal team was still grinding away trying to get the organization to pivot and adjust and was about *halfway through its new procedures*, we had already confirmed that our product was safe, of the highest quality, and that it possessed all of the other characteristics that make a great deliverable. We helped our client move faster so they could stick to what they do well.

As of this writing, this head-to-head experiment is just about to end, and the scenario we presented performed so well that the CPG company is currently reassessing whether or not they will continue using internal teams to validate small-scale co-manufacturers.

The key insight to realize is that in the qualification process for co-manufacturers, CPG companies establish a high bar for the volume of production, level of experience, and degrees of safety and risk mitigation. And while these standards are very beneficial (especially for maintaining safety), the internally developed criteria usually end up doing little more than creating a validation structure that only approves of those large co-manufacturers who are already partnered with the company. It's almost like an inward-looking set of criteria that only defines acceptable risk as the framework that already exists. In this system, very few other production facilities ultimately live up to qualifications that were designed with existing partners in mind.

Unfortunately, the exclusivity of the process can close the door on opportunities to partner with exciting new manufacturing startups, or even larger co-manufacturers who have been around for decades but just haven't yet had the chance to work with a Fortune 500 CPG company.

The *Make* model requires a certain amount of entrepreneurial freedom to locate a suitable production facility, connect with creative new partners, and brainstorm new ways to produce a limited number of units with market-ready quality.

In matching rigor to risk, we often mitigate concerns in alternative and entrepreneurial ways, such as by focusing on testing thoroughly during and after production to ensure quality is at the required levels. This can help provide confidence in both the quality and safety of the finished goods.

When we help clients with *Make,* our role is to de-risk the project by taking the ownership and assuming all liability that anything we make and test will be safe and effective. Quality and consumer safety always remain priority number one. Since we are capable of owning the risk of the small manufacturing run, and can manage the safety and quality with third-party vendors, clients can focus solely on the insights and how those insights can guide their organization for large-scale execution.

3. SCALE OR BAIL

With *Make,* we don't seek to perfect the short-term manufacturing process. There's no need for that *before* you have proven if an innovation is even worthwhile. It is more about the next level of proof of your elevated MVP. We are still in the process of prescale proof-of-concept. We want a line of sight to the future production process, not an exact replication of a perfect process.

For example, if it costs tens of thousands of dollars to install a machine at a small co-manufacturer that shakes seeds onto the tops of granola bars, we would recommend creating a temporary shortcut with a handful of people shaking the seeds out with wire screens. If there is a need to create a fast, entrepreneurial, or low-budget workaround, then focus on ensuring there is a valid scaled version via equipment that can be used on a production line to produce the same result on a bigger scale in the future.

The advantage of this model is that it gives you the opportunity to "scale or bail" with bailing out being the operative response. Recall the insight from Clayton Christensen and others that between 70 and 90 percent of new products fail. If everything has to be perfected *before being tested*, and a large proportion of what is tested will be worthless, then it will always seem onerous to test anything if perfection in manufacturing is the goal.

Just like it's important (and easy) to iterate with the nuggets of a concept, it should also be important (and easy) to iterate with the production of something new before you fully commit to it. Yes, you always want to make products at a high fidelity that consumers will appreciate, but there also needs to be room for improvement. The perfection in manufacturing can and should come after the idea has been validated. That's when the beauty of a large CPG can take over and do its scaled magic.

4. TO GO BIG, THINK SMALL

When it comes to finding the right production partner, sometimes it's necessary to look in unusual places. Everyone thinks of manufacturing options as coming from your standard factories, but one of the more unique types of food-producing partners we've found is located on college campuses. The food-science and dairy departments on university campuses are just one example of groups that have worked with us to make innovative ideas come to life.

These departments are very happy to let you work with them to utilize their equipment. It's hard to simulate the intense heat and pressure that modern retort processing does to canned foods, and that equipment is not lying around in your average R&D lab. But if you know where to look, you can partner with a university's retort equipment to Battle Test™ your new formula.

Beyond universities, small startups, international co-manufacturers, and even emerging entrepreneurs can also be great resources. With these alternative resources, it's not about the efficiency or the volume of output but about the co-manufacturer being curious and having excitement and comfort about learning and experimenting with new ideas.

Another key to working with small operations is to make sure that they want to play and have fun. Developing a new item takes trial and error, and groups that are operationalized for efficiency and volume usually don't have the time and patience to try out a new idea. The ultimate goal is to create a win-win between large CPG companies and smaller, creative co-manufacturers.

There are other scenarios in *Make* that benefit from a quicker, more nimble outside organization. An example of this is when a company seeks information from in-house legal or regulatory departments during the innovation process.

Large CPG companies generally have powerful teams of lawyers that are well-versed in every state and federal regulation. They're outstanding at protecting the company and serving as an advocate for consumer safety and quality. Unfortunately, because these legal teams tend to address higher-order priorities and have volumes of work to manage, the time it takes for them to engage internally with a new-product team can sometimes be months. Even a simple query about wording for packaging can take several weeks—a delay that can grind a fast-paced innovation process to a halt.

Whether it's outsourcing legal opinions or procuring hard-to-get items in the supply chain, the *Make* process detours around these common sources of delay. *Make* is a flexible process that can apply to a broad range of challenges, from the most daunting project to the simplest of assignments. The *Make* model can help design an entire manufacturing process from scratch, assisting with every step even down to the ordering of ingredients. But it can also tackle the smaller tasks that big companies aren't equipped to address, such as repackaging a product with a new label for a thousand-unit test.

5. SCALING UP THE ENTREPRENEURIAL MODEL

There's a whole network of manufacturers who know how to do small, innovative production. They might not be suitable for mass-manufacturing, but they can help test disruptive ideas on a small scale and bring your idea to life to see if it has legs with real consumers.

Regardless of the size of your company or the guardrails that might exist internally, for the purposes of innovation and pushing boundaries, you don't need to be constrained by what you *can* or *cannot* do today. The *Make* process finds a way to create a product with three goals in mind:

- Seeing if it works

- Proving that it can be done later on a bigger scale

- Doing so safely

INSIGHT: In all of this talk about innovation, do you feel left behind? Don't worry, a 2020 KPMG study found that 60 percent of executives believed their innovation efforts were at the earliest stages of development (ad hoc or emerging) while only 2 percent felt they were at the highest level and "optimized."[26]

In a sense, *Make* is just the scaled-up version of an entrepreneurial model. Think about the one-person operation where an entrepreneur comes up with a cool idea, makes a little in their kitchen, and hands it out to friends. When it gets a positive

---

26 Innovation Leader and KPMG LLC, *Benchmarking Innovation Impact 2020* (2019), https://info.kpmg.us/content/dam/info/en/innovation-enterprise-solutions/pdf/2019/benchmarking-innovation-impact-2020.pdf.

reception, they rent a commercial kitchen, make a little more, and sell it at a local farmer's market. With each new round of production, the operation grows and iteration continues until the product is consumer optimized.

We're starting to see this thinking take hold in a handful of our larger CPG clients. But the lesson they are internalizing is important, as they are learning that launches don't always have to be about getting to 85 percent ACV in the first few months. They are starting to understand that there is power in the entrepreneurial model in scaling production only after you have scaled demand.

This is how we broke boundaries at OxiClean. We would often launch an idea in a small way and let the consumer demand build slowly over time for anywhere between nine months to eighteen months. While that demand slowly rose, we got better at manufacturing: better quality, better cost controls, faster production, and more. Then, after seeing it advertised direct-to-consumer for close to a year, we would have retailers start to *ask us* when they would be able to get that new product we'd just launched.

QUOTE: *"I have a desire to teach my organization to have patience in building demand before trying to build supply. We need to reframe our innovation efforts as growing demand first while slowly building supply to keep up. This thinking is the opposite of what we do today because our launch model is all about building massive amounts of national supply then trying* *to drive enough demand to make that all worthwhile. This new way is better because it de-risks an innovative launch, especially before we invest $20 to $30 million in capital for mass-scaled production."*

—INNOVATION VP, large CPG

No entrepreneur gets rich from a great idea without actually doing something with it. Once they've figured out how to manufacture their great idea, they need to try it out in the real world. It's time to *Burst* into transactional testing.

CHAPTER EIGHT

TRANSACTIONAL TESTING: BURST

You have to dream it. You also have to make it. But you're not really done with a new innovation until you *sell* it. You have to put your product on shelves and see if consumers will purchase it in a real-world environment. Only then do you know if you're on to something big.

We've seen many promising innovations fall short because a CPG company evaluated an idea primarily on a computer screen or in some kind of simulation. During testing consumers reacted positively to the idea, *saying* that they would purchase it. However, when the product was launched and consumers moved from saying to *doing* through their shopping behaviors, in the context of their real and full lives, the favorable test results didn't translate into sales and the launch underachieved its goals.

INSIGHT: People vote with their wallets™ one purchasing decision at a time.

The atmosphere in a retail store—a supermarket, a convenience store, a home-and-hardware chain, a quick-serve restaurant, a pet store—with all of its competitive noise and distractions, with its 30,000, 60,000, or 120,000 available options, with promotions and sale prices, and new items staring you in your face, is all wildly different from an online study or focus-group environment. While we're big believers in the value and focused role of qualitative research and quantitative studies, there is simply *no way* that any *simulated* model can truly replicate the in-store consumer purchasing behavior that is critical to understand an innovation's true potential—be it good or bad.

With the *Burst* transactional testing model, we are proposing a holistic, fast-paced, real-world, and entrepreneurial approach: make a little, *sell a little*, learn a lot. It's grounded in bringing the total proposition to consumers, in context and with real-world pressures. It's about having consumers "show you, not tell you." And it can enable you to learn, pivot, and iterate before scaling ideas up.

Burst transactional testing can de-risk both new product innovations and existing product renovations and can be executed in any number of retail spaces to meet your objectives. Coupled with a process that deeply analyzes shopper behavior, competitive sales through point of sale (POS) data, shopper card data, interviews, and more, the insights become incredibly powerful, actionable, and projectible in a way that can't compare to any simulated test of behavior.

INSIGHT: The EMBR philosophy is fundamentally a comprehensive validation process and is dedicated to ending all of the various disconnects in CPG innovation processes.

To understand *Burst,* we first have to delve into the background of transactional testing.

BOOM, SPLAT

The "boom, splat" launch is a far-too-common phenomenon in big CPG companies. Characterized by high hopes and expectations based on rave reviews in multiple simulated consumer tests, a "boom, splat" launch is usually supported by strong marketing and go-to-market plans that turn into lackluster results on the shelves and end in discontinuation within one to three years. This kind of launch becomes a very expensive endeavor in terms of lost time, revenue, and opportunity cost, not to mention unhappy retail partners and missed internal projections for growth.

The "boom, splat" pattern is a tremendous source of ongoing frustration, and culturally, it can result in debilitating fear of failure and paralysis. But *the industry-standard tools used today can and do miss in their predictions of success.* If that was not the case, then 70 to 90 percent of new product launches wouldn't be failing year after year. We are only blinding ourselves to reality if we ignore this fact.

> **INSIGHT:** According to company legend (verified by some back-of-the-envelope math), a deck passed around at P&G revealed that one of the factors that caused a new brand to be shuttered a few years after launching with more than $100 million in support—a classic "boom, splat"—was, as one slide put it, "We would have made more money for the company if we'd put all the cash spent on marketing and promotion into buying the product and then distributing it for free."

Our experience, validated through many, many client discussions, indicates that simulated tests of consumer interest and behavior have various levels of inaccuracies at predicting in-market success. The following are a few key reasons why:

1) Disruptive Innovations Are Hard to Test Conceptually. The more radical and disruptive an idea is, the harder it is to communicate that product in a concept test. As a result, many simulated tests overcommunicate the proposition, benefits, and/ or claims to try to bring the idea to life. When the product is fully developed and the true limitations are in place—such as the small real estate on a package label, limited space to make claims, maybe legal restrictions for what claims are allowed to be placed on the product or in the marketing campaign—the consumer will likely not get the same level of communication that was shared in a focus-group room on a 2D digital concept page. At shelf, the product may struggle with the intangibility of what it is, as disruptive innovations often require new behaviors and additional education. The consumer may simply not know what to do with it, how to use it, or where it fits in their lives.

2) The Noncommittal Nature of Simulations. Clients have repeatedly told us how often premium and higher-priced items get winning scores in concept screens then fail to sell at shelf. Partly, this seems to be because a high price point (perhaps greater than five dollars per unit, or greater than thirty dollars per unit) is easy to commit to in a test when no money is actually exchanged, but it takes real time and commitment for a consumer to make a buying decision in a store when their hard-earned money is on the line. Partly, this also stems from the fact that there are often no real comparisons during the test. In a store, the consumer can easily shift their gaze to the next dozen similar items and find the promise and price point that works for them.

3) Lack of Reality. Concept tests and shopping simulations just can't replicate the real-life scenario of a mom or dad with a kid tugging at their hem, needing to grab a family favorite or find a new product and move on. It also misses the reality of the consumer needing to balance spending with real-world alternatives, a total budget, or a values-based philosophy. A retailer's shelf is, in many cases, the first moment of truth for consumers—the first time they are exposed to a product line—and it needs to stand out from distractions, competitors, and more.

4) Executing What Was Tested. What is tested is not always what launches. Perhaps a well-meaning marketer gamed the system to get the best results at each stage of testing. Or the simulated go-to-market plan's promotion and communication wound up different at the time of launch. Or maybe the wording in the concept overpromised the ability for R&D to deliver. It all comes down to "garbage in, garbage out."

Our history of measuring the results on innovation transactional tests has begun to validate where concept testing *alone* does not always compare to real-world results. The more we test our clients' concept-validated (e.g., high concept score) ideas, the more we see that concept tests are not always guaranteed to be predictors of in-market success.

Allow us to prove why.

In Figure A, you'll see a trinomial (three-hump) curve based on more than several hundred in-market innovation tests we've performed on behalf of clients. The X-axis represents the overall success rating (performance of the item versus its competitive set on a scale of 0 to 100), using real in-market transactional results. The Y-axis represents the percentage of all tests that fall into each point (the space below the line) of ranked in-market performance.

You might expect the distribution to look like a standard bell curve: one peak with many tests that are average, some outperforming, and some falling short. It's also reasonable to expect that the center of the bell curve would be above the 50 percent mark. After all, these ideas have been vigorously studied and validated in concept tests, consumer qualitative tests, and more, so they should have an above-average chance of outperforming their categories. To some extent, this is true with the highest point of the curve to the right, since its center point shows that the median of that distribution of tests falls above the 70 percent mark (a solidly above-average result).

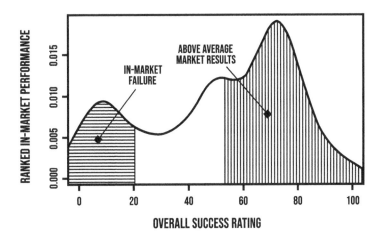

Figure A

But what about the smallest curve to the left, the one with its high point around 9 percent that represents a notable percentage of all tests performed? What's going on there? That curve represents winning concept tests being smacked in the face with the reality of in-market failure. They represent the shocking performance of successful concept tests underperforming against their existing competitive set. The insight should be clear—**positive concept test results do not guarantee in-market success**.

The *Burst* model is designed to help address this type of shortfall. Instead of spending three to five years of time and resources launching an idea that has only been tested "theoretically" or in discrete pieces and components, *Burst* allows a disruptive innovation to be tested holistically, in a real competitive selling market— all meant to generate insights before reaching the internal stage gate that ramps the whole company up to full launch mode.

THE SUPERMARKET JUNGLE

There's another reason simulated testing isn't a great predictor of on-shelf success. In the real world, a typical supermarket might contain sixty thousand or more individual stock-keeping units (SKUs). The sheer number of decisions facing a shopper in a grocery store is staggering. In this supermarket jungle, a new product needs to break through, communicating something new, interesting, or different in split seconds. Regardless of how amazing the product inside the package is, it simply won't make it into a shopper's cart unless it stands out on a shelf to all types of shoppers, whether they are distracted, hyperfocused, or pursuing a list-based pattern of buying.

A shopper in a store behaves differently than a consumer at home watching TV or surfing the internet. When consumers encounter broad-based advertising, they might actually take a moment to consider the product and its message. But consumers watching an ad are also weighing the product independently, not against its hundreds of competitors. The same is true for consumers in simulated product testing. They are forced to consider a product idea in a vacuum (likely monadically), without the vast wealth of competition present in a supermarket. Shoppers, on the other hand, must make split-second decisions in the retail jungle, often in the midst of a series of errands, sometimes hungry or simply rushed.

QUOTE: *"I think every marketer should have to go do a grocery-shopping trip on their way home from work with a toddler or two that they just picked up from daycare to really understand the distracted shopper experience that many of our target consumers live with all the time. I mean, how many products aren't targeted at or being bought primarily by moms between the ages of twenty-five to forty-nine?"*

—CARAGH MCLAUGHLIN,
Managing Director, Mission Field®

This fundamental difference between *consumer* insights and *shopper* insights can produce misleading results in concept testing. Consumers will give one response in a simulation, and then behave quite differently in a store. In our many years of consumer research, we have consistently seen inflated numbers in response to common questions such as, "Will this item replace your existing products?" or "Will this be something new in addition to what you already use?"

A two-hour focus-group discussion about everyday household goods is great for fleshing out options, ranking good versus bad ideas, and testing how far those possibilities can go, but it's bad for understanding true purchasing behavior. When a consumer spends more than an hour focused on one product in a focus group—a brand of cereal, for example—it can be easy to watch them shift from *like* to *love* and get caught in the upswell of group dynamics. And while they may swear that they'll add that cereal to their repertoire of purchases, it doesn't always play out that way in real life.

When the consumer gets to a store and becomes a *shopper*, a different mindset takes hold. In the cereal aisle of a large retailer, a shopper is facing a task list of over fifty items to purchase and the need to find the next one or two among a forty-foot shelf containing upwards of one thousand individual SKUs. If a new product's package isn't distinctive and compelling, if the packaging doesn't clearly communicate a story, purpose, and benefit, if the box is in a different place than the shopper is searching, or if the product looks too simple or too complex, an amazing idea can meet an untimely death and be overlooked for the products the shopper already buys regularly. In the end, the result might be the exact opposite of what a focus group predicted would happen.

That split-second decision in the store often has nothing to do with the quality of the idea. A consumer may love the idea of a new food or beverage and may think that it's mind-blowing and amazing. In a focus group, or even an in-home product test, the consumer may give it an unreserved thumbs-up. But then when the consumer becomes a shopper in the grocery aisle, they may avoid the new product because it looks *too damn good.*

Perhaps the shopper is middle-aged and has started to think more about what they eat. They're considering more than just great taste. In a taste test, they aren't thinking about how the product fits in with an overall diet, but in the store, when they add it to a pile of other foods, they start to second-guess how it fits with their life goals.

That kind of bias is only revealed when a person is in the store deciding what to take home for themselves or their family. All other hypothetical thinking they provided in qualitative research, or the purchase-interest rating they gave it on a concept test, is all flawed information to some degree. The only feedback that's actually important is *the behavior they exhibit* amongst hundreds of items competing for their dollars, time, or caloric budget.

CASE: We tested an innovative new product for a client that was backed by a considerable amount of food development research and insight generation. Their concept was sound, tasted great, and was on-trend as it was about making healthier foods more approachable and interesting. Their talented designers created truly beautiful packaging with a distinctive ethos and a unique package structure.

Unfortunately, when the product was placed on-shelf, we quickly found out that shoppers couldn't read the label. The images on the package looked outstanding and breakthrough on a computer screen, but when reduced to the life-size package label, they were hard to interpret. To make matters worse, the people who were most interested in the product were over fifty and mostly needed glasses. And not everyone brings their reading glasses to the store!

> Since the label was hard to read and the packaging structure was unique, many shoppers overlooked the product because they could not easily understand what it was or how it fit in their lives, and they missed the opportunity to try an innovative and delicious new offering. This transactional test led to deep learnings and opportunities to improve the offering before a major launch.

The best way to overcome the limitations of concept and simulation testing is to sell your idea in the real world—in the jungle of the supermarket, the pet store, the hardware store, or the food-service operator—where a consumer *has no other choice* but to vote with their wallets™. A purchase of your product is a vote for your idea. A purchase of the competitor's product is a rejection (or at least, a noncommitment) of your idea. This is fairly simple and a much more accurate way to predict success. It's important to recognize that "failure" in a transactional test that captures a chance to optimize or pivot for a future launch should be seen as time and money well spent—risk mitigation, not failure!

THE RETAILER TESTING CONUNDRUM

Any retail chain out there—Walmart, Kroger, Target, Home Depot, Walgreens, 7-Eleven, PetSmart, GNC, Ulta Beauty—is run by buyers and category managers, and those key decision-makers have thousands of manufacturers, both big and small, fighting to meet with them to discuss their product lines. So even big, powerful CPG companies like Procter & Gamble, Nestlé, Hershey's, or

Clorox can claim only a precious few moments with buyers per month or per quarter.

It's not uncommon for a manufacturer's salesperson to get only a one-hour meeting with a buyer, and in that hour, the salesperson will be hoping to cover ten critically important sales issues, another five topics that are somewhat pressing, and another dozen agenda items that they'd love to bring up but will never have the time to fully address.

On top of that, a salesperson in the beauty-care unit at P&G might represent fifteen or more brands at any given time. By the time each of those brands adds a stack of decks for a sales meeting, there might be a physical *tower* of material that the salesperson is expected to present.

With such limited time, they are forced to focus on only the most important components of the job: listening to the retailer's needs and objectives, making sure the supply chain needs of the retailer are properly serviced, confirming that the retailer has scheduled their brands and category's upcoming promotions, and advocating for a fair share of shelf space and positioning. The salesperson also has their own sales objectives and naturally focuses on the biggest parts of the business in order to hit their annual goals.

Meanwhile, the buyer may have their own focus, and they need to discuss the retailer's eternal quest for 99.7 percent on-time delivery from each manufacturer. So when can the salesperson get around to pitching a way to test their disruptive new ideas? Often, they don't. They can't. They shouldn't. It's just not feasible.

Even if a salesperson *did* have time to pitch a test of new product ideas, and even if they *could* arrange a small in-store trial, it would be a high-risk proposition. If a new idea hits the shelves at a big retail chain (even in just a handful of stores) and *fails*, the CPG company will face a big challenge in bringing it back to the retail chain. The retailer will have already seen the idea fail and won't want to see it again. When a product test originates directly from a CPG company, it often has one shot at success. If the failed test occurs with one of the company's top three retail partners, they've potentially forfeited up to 30 percent of a product's total sales volume. That bridge is burned.

TESTING YOUR OBJECTIVES

The key to any kind of transactional test is to first understand and define your key insight objectives. At the simplest level, there are different ways to test a new innovation (a new brand or an extension of an existing brand) or a renovation of an existing, sizable brand. But it has to go further than that. A transactional test needs to get clear what exactly it is that you are trying to learn because that insight-objective focus will define and shape the test's design and how you move forward from there.

For new innovations, you can consider which of the following insight objectives is your primary objective:

- Understanding a volumetric number for a "size of the prize" build

- Testing the A/B impact of specific pricing, positioning, or other key variables

- Iterative learning that refines and optimizes the proposition holistically

- Building a sales story to help convince a retailer your item is worth supporting

- Checking your gut intuition to frame future development work

For renovations of existing—and especially large-volume or high-profit brands—the focus can be one of many different key insight variables such as:

- Statistically evaluating the sales impact of an overt change to the brand

- Evaluating a blinded or hidden change or an unannounced upgrade

- Identifying the interaction potential between your renovation and your larger portfolio

- Measuring the overall impact of one or many changes to the bottom line (profit)

- Assessing the possibility of a renovation satisfying new or current target audiences

- Clarifying the executional back-room/back-of-house use of the new variants

No matter what you are trying to measure, the importance of the brand to the business means testing must read the impact of a potential change with a high level of sensitivity so as to detect a true positive result and avoid statistical false negatives or false positives.

TESTING FOR YOUR FUTURE

Recently, many big CPG companies have been contemplating how they might use Amazon or social selling as a testing platform before launching a product at scale in traditional retail. Interestingly, entrepreneurs do this often and quite successfully for testing as a way of identifying their top products to expand to retail. They effectively learn and iterate online, then grow those products in retail—but at an entrepreneur's pace and scale, not as a national "we have it all dialed in" launch.

While we support, and often execute, transactional tests online, we also caution our large CPG clients to clarify and understand their key business objectives, specifically, **"Where do you plan to build your business?"**

Amazon-based testing can help flush out insights, test communications, provide prioritization and more, but what it is not going to do is be a predictor of the volumetrics of a new product in a brick-and-mortar retail environment, the place where 85 to 90 percent of the volume of a large CPG brand is sold.[27]

The best way to help de-risk and validate your innovation is to design a test that links to both your *insight objective* and your *business objective*. So, if you're hoping to establish your brand by selling in college campus bookstores, you are best served by testing your product *on a college campus*. If you want to launch something cool in the food-service channel and coffee shops, then you should test *in coffee shops*. If the lion's share of your business is going to come from selling the product in the grocery channel, you need to test *in the grocery channel*. It's all about gathering the metrics and building the right business based on shopper behavior from the place where you plan to succeed.

RIGHT SIZING THE EFFORT

We believe in the critical importance of transactional testing to validate products before large-scale launches. That said, the ideal is to start with a small-scale test launch—a toe in the water, so to speak, to assess product performance on the shelf with shoppers.

27   Russel Redman, "Grocery Retail Sales Climb 7.5% in September," Supermarket News, October 15, 2021, https://www.supermarketnews.com/retail-financial/grocery-retail-sales-climb-75-september; Statista Research Department, "Online Grocery Shopping Sales in the United States from 2019 to 2024," Statista, January 27, 2022, https://www.statista.com/statistics/293707/us-online-grocery-sales.

Big CPG companies can sell in the real world, of course, but as we previously discussed in-depth in part one of this book, they are designed to produce on a massive scale for all the right reasons. We empathize and understand that it can be challenging to execute a product test in only a dozen stores that represents a 0.012 percent ACV (all commodity volume) launch. A launch of any size is complex and takes a lot of effort to organize.

Ultimately, we believe that the most effective way to properly evaluate and de-risk any kind of new product launch is to "make a little and sell a little™" in the space and place where you plan to launch. We want you, with this transactional testing step, to build confidence in the idea within the organization. This is the core of the entrepreneurial approach of *Burst. Burst* tests ultimately give you the *agility* of an entrepreneur. Whether it's food, drug, mass, club, pet, pet specialty, hardware, convenience, food service, or any other channel—test where your future is focused at the smallest scale that gives you the confidence your team requires.

THE BURST MODEL

Now that we have covered some of the insights into why it's hard but important for large CPG companies to do transactional testing, it's worth thinking about the spectrum of testing that *can* occur. There's more than one option available, depending on your readiness status, timing, and insight objectives.

Continuum of Burst Testing

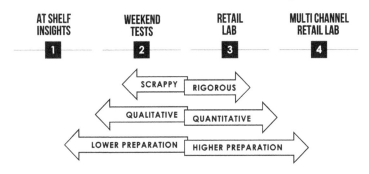

1. At-Shelf Insights (ASI)

At-Shelf Insights (ASI)™ is a fast, scrappy, qualitative method of testing the basic viability of a concept on a store shelf, even before you have a sellable final product. Our methodology uses recruited consumers to learn about and optimize the concept in-store.

ASI is the perfect testing methodology for big CPG companies that may have a great idea but want to test the impact of the concept in the real world without needing to fully build it out. Perhaps the R&D department is still perfecting the formula, or there are multiple ways to approach the concept and it's unclear which version will break through.

ASI allows the shopper to make an in-store decision and judge the idea qualitatively against the wealth of other available options on the shelf. Remember the "retail jungle" that we discussed earlier? This test is an excellent quick measure of whether or not an idea stands out in that competitive retail environment and makes an impact. You are able to get useful feedback from dozens of consumers in a very short timeframe and begin assessing whether or not your concept has traction.

In a recent ASI project, we were able to help a client test their idea against a range of other competitors. Through that effort, we learned that the concept did well overall but not as well as expected because the competitive dynamics were tougher than the client realized. We also learned that the pricing could come up—a nice win—but that the label needed more clarity if it was going to make an impact. All of this would have been hard to achieve in a standard focus-group facility.

2. Weekend Tests

While still a somewhat scrappy, agile form of testing, weekend tests are a more in-depth method of obtaining consumer reactions to a more complete proposition, especially one that is demonstrable and experiential (it can be shown, sampled, or demonstrated). While an ASI test collects dozens of consumer responses to a rough idea, weekend tests can garner feedback from *hundreds* of shoppers on the entire holistic proposition. Weekend tests also add a *quantitative* layer to the qualitative information gained through various KPIs (key performance indicators) that can be used to evaluate success against past weekend tests.

Weekend tests are highly *iterative* in nature because they allow you a chance to play with positioning, pricing, formula, packaging, and communication approaches, but they also offer an extra strategic lens that can help *triangulate* key business insights that might impact the next steps an innovation team can take on the opportunity. Business insights that can be collected include exploring the dynamics of the same idea in different channels, in different geographies, even with different competitive sets.

Through the weekend test process, you can narrow in on the target audience by identifying the demographics and psychographics of interested buyers, interested nonbuyers, and rejectors. You can also learn which types of consumer falls into each category and start building a quantitative database of norms for the number and types of consumers who express interest and why.

A weekend test is also great for training the innovation team's guts—their marketing guts, their insight guts, their "what matters" guts. Sometimes, with all the strategy work and all the decks written, a team just needs to get in the field and hear the voice of the consumer to bring to life and refine what they already know. There's nothing better for the core team than to *stop thinking about the theory and hear from shoppers and store personnel* about why the idea works, or doesn't work.

In one weekend test experience a few years ago, a client's key R&D person joined a research event in a natural-leaning pet store, where they were trying to sell an innovative twist on a conventional pet food brand. While there, the R&D person had consumer after consumer tell him how his well-known brand of pet food had ingredients in it that they felt were risky and could be harmful to their pets.

In some discussions, consumers would stay at the booth and talk for up to twenty minutes about their perceptions and beliefs. After the tenth or eleventh customer did this, the R&D manager turned to me and said, "None of them were incorrect in their expression of the science." Although he felt they were overprojecting the impact, he was floored mostly because he hadn't fully understood the level of knowledge held by their target consumer, *even though he had read plenty of studies that told him this fact*. The weekend test brought to life something he intellectually understood but hadn't intuitively comprehended, and it helped inform the next iteration of the project.

3. Retail Labs

The retail lab is where an innovation team's proverbial rubber hits the road. It's the gold standard for organizations wishing to rigorously and comprehensively understand the scope and scale of their proposition. The retail lab takes more preparation to set up, but its output is designed to deliver key datasets that can validate the primary insight objectives and business metrics of a new innovative idea, a critical brand renovation, or a shift in strategy— all built on the back of thousands of test item sales versus tens of thousands of competitive item sales. In the end, the idea behind retail labs is to test your opportunity against real consumer behavior. There's no debate that the purchasing patterns in a store connect directly to actual consumer shopping behavior.

The way all this data comes together allows you to model the future of what your innovation's impact will be on its category. Keep in mind that a retail lab can be set up with a variety of objectives: from a quick gut check, to iterative optimization, the building of volumetrics and projections, or an in-depth and highly accurate renovation change.

- **Innovations and Iterative Optimization.** These tests are designed to allow you to play with all of the dimensions of the innovation in order to optimize it for its future launch state. This could involve A/B testing different strategic communication, prices, positioning, placement, branding, or a host of other opportunities. The main goal is to use the real selling data of a test to help clarify the *impact* of the factors being studied and guide you to a more optimized solution prior to a launch.

- **Innovations and Volumetrics/Projectability.** These tests are designed to validate the questions, "Do I have a winning idea?" and "How big is big?" They start with the assumption that the innovation team has nailed the main components, and now it's time to put it to the test to provide in-market proof for the internal organization ahead of a scaled launch. These tests compare the predicted sales volume of a product to the volume of its competitors and help to frame the projections for what might happen at launch. They help identify significance.

- **Renovation Assessments.** This type of test starts with an existing brand in mind and asks: "If I change X, Y, or even A though G, what will happen? Will I positively or negatively affect my business?" Tests of renovation are fundamentally different than tests of innovations because the design, scale, and output need to take into account how changes will affect a core business. And when you're talking about one of your billion-dollar brands, testing is critical because each 0.5 percent impact can be significant to the bottom line.

Retail labs are about quantitative learnings, but they can go much further. It starts with collecting key data and metrics through point-of-sale transactions on everything, including dollar and unit sales, dollar and unit share, changes between test and control cells, category impact, and so much more. In channels and retailers that have shopper card data, you get into even deeper metrics such as trial, repeat, source of volume, incrementality, market basket, household profiles, and many other key business-metric data points.

We then recommend layering qualitative measures through in-store research, interviews, and more to ensure that you understand the *why* behind the data-based *what*. Add in the ability to execute marketing mix analysis, "size of the prize" analysis (including top-down, bottom-up, and pro-forma designs), normative testing, and retailer interviews, and you have a powerful system to validate your products and concepts.

One distinct advantage of conducting a retail lab in stores is that it's possible to gauge repeat purchasing behavior. Most tests can detect consumer interest in an idea, but CPG companies are looking for consumers to continually purchase their products. Testing for repeat purchasing can't be done with an online screen test, a virtual shopping shelf, or an idea statement. It can only be accomplished by putting your product in stores, selling it through multiple repeat cycles, and measuring what happens. The data analysis in the *Burst* process can reveal whether or not a new product will become part of a consumer's regular routine.

Burst analysis can also predict how a consumer's purchase will affect other products' sales in the category. That way, you can determine if the purchase was incremental to the category (i.e., someone adding the product to their basket on top of the products they already buy), or if the purchase was incremental to your brand by taking business away from a competitor. You can also establish whether a given purchase cannibalized sales of your own products, and if so, if a brand switch will help or hurt overall profits at your CPG company.

We recommend executing a level of marketing support just as you would do at launch, including a level of support that mimics and matches what your company would typically recommend for their new-product launch model. This might be a mix of in-store activity, such as price discounting, displays, endcaps, shelf programs, retailer programs, and more. It can also mean out-of-store communication such as geo-targeted digital campaigns, coupons, TV, print, radio, and even out-of-store sampling events. The main goal of this is to mimic exactly what you would do at launch so you're guaranteed to see the real impact of those efforts on the test of a new innovation.

The traditional approach to in-market tests is to conduct one large enough that it can deal with errors in the data such as stock outages, shelf inaccuracies, variances across different store's sell-through rates, and more. However, it's hard to control a myriad of things across a wide range of disconnected stores. It is more accurate, and better for testing, to use a carefully designed, statistically optimized, and tightly controlled approach in which a careful connection with the retailer is of the utmost importance.

As discussed earlier, we find that most large CPG companies find it challenging to set up a test like this internally. It can help to use a third party to set up the retailer, expedite logistics, and externalize the pain points associated with the small-scale testing operations not inherently built into the company's day-to-day operations, such as servicing a small number of stores, setting up all the details in the retailer system, expediting UPC codes, and managing qualified direct store delivery (DSD) staff for the duration of the test to ensure data accuracy and implement any pivots needed to optimize the test.

Whether or not you use an outside third party, **retail labs provide a much more quantitative way of allowing an organization to fully understand the impact of a new idea backed by real shopper behavior—not modeled or interpreted consumer analysis, but real in-store consumer behavior.**

Online Retail Labs

We wrote earlier about the importance of testing in the channel(s) *where* your future business plans to be. With the continued rise of online shopping, including food, home goods, pet, and more, a growing number of companies will want to test online for the future of their significant or growing online businesses. Amazon, direct-to-consumer (DTC) sites, social selling (selling products through social media outlets like Facebook and TikTok), and other online retailers will only continue to grow in importance.

At its core, an online retail lab can be very powerful, efficient, and effective. There are obvious benefits in that the logistics and executional complexities of setting up a website or selling through Amazon can be significantly less onerous than the equivalent setup for a brick-and-mortar location. You can also execute an online test with a fairly small number of sellable units, *and* you can pivot and test alternative communication points and iterations at lightning speed. Like the offline retail lab, the power comes in moving from simulations to actual qualitative learnings tied to consumers' *doing* behavior—shopping with real dollars for a real product.

Executing an online retail lab requires understanding the differences versus traditional CPG testing and optimizing the test to gain the most of the medium. Shopping behavior, competitive context, and advertising are radically different from the equivalent traditional in-person versions. Not better or worse, just different, and with different executional priorities, metrics, and competitive pressures.

No doubt, selling online, and specifically through Amazon as a retailer, is strategically important to many brands. We have seen retail buyers pull up a company's Amazon product reviews and performance before committing to a buy. We've helped clients use Amazon and DTC sites as a way to learn, iterate, and strengthen new ideas in the real world.

4. Multichannel Retail Labs

Multichannel retail labs are the highest level of sales assessment before a full nationwide product launch, taking the quantitative rigor of a retail lab and multiplying it across numerous sales channels in varied geographies at the same time. Despite the enormity of the trial, you should be able to tweak, edit, and adjust the idea as the process unfolds. Multichannel retail labs take testing to an even higher level of statistical validation and can predict the "size of the prize" with the highest level of confidence. At this volume of testing, the statistical findings are almost undebatable.

SELECTING FROM THE SPECTRUM

The "closer-in" ideas emerging from CPG companies may require less rigorous testing, but the farther out ideas will undoubtedly require more rigorous tests and quantitative analysis. And the ideas that are unprecedented, or that require completely new consumer behaviors, need the *Burst* process most of all. Regardless, all of them will benefit from the holistic nature of *Burst*.

A hypothetical and disruptive new cleaning product that challenges consumers to adopt a completely new approach to a household task ("Am I dusting? Am I sweeping? What am I doing?") simply isn't going to be as compatible with the industry-standard models of concept testing. Radical new ideas that are asking for changes in consumer behavior compel us to engage the in-depth testing, iteration, and shopping behavior insights built into the *Burst* model to help prove them out.

THE POWER OF A NORMATIVE DATABASE: FACTORS OF SUCCESS

Over Mission Field®'s history of executing several hundred retail labs that output quantitative results, we have been able to statistically model data from each of those different tests and compare each one against each other to create a baseline of "normative data." You can think of it as a database by which you can compare future tests against to validate success as we showed in Figure A earlier in this chapter. But what also makes this data fascinating is that it is not only a measurement of the performance of test products, but also a measurement of every competitive item being sold for the year prior to the introduction of those test items and during the time of their test—and the *factors* of success that we can derive from studying that database.

Using advanced machine learning models to model what "success" looks like for disruptive ideas, new brands, existing brand line extensions, and innovations in different product categories, we have come up with multiple key factors that help determine the success for new innovation:

- **Impact.** The *Impact* of a product is measured by its percentile of cumulative performance relative to comparable items. This key factor is calculated based on cumulative sales, separately for units and revenue, and is modeled to be comparable across similar testing circumstances. While we see many high-performing tests of innovation perform at high levels, it is sometimes OK for a high-performing product to be in the middle of its pack. So when launching a new innovation, you don't always need to be a leader in sales; you can often be a high performer with a "good starting point."

- **Grippiness.** The *Grippiness* of a product is a measure of its intermediate and ongoing performance after key promotional support periods have been taken into account. To help avoid the "boom, splat" effect that some product launches have in the real world, and to take into account the need for promotional rhythms that keep products on the shelf and in the right competitive context, Grippiness clarifies the product's potential to be a long-term growth play and not a flash in the pan. What innovators need to understand is that promotions are a two-sided coin: overdoing the promotional efforts in a testing can juice results and skew your data, but the lack of promotional support can also undermine your test. The modeling of Grippiness helps to clarify an innovation's potential to stay on the shelf even with promotions happening around it and to it.

- **Range.** The *Range* of a product is a measure of its floor and ceiling of sales and is meant to convey both the downside risks and upside potential of a product, highlighted by its different extremes in a mathematical context. This testing is modeled relative to comparable products and is focused on results in a very specific time period of the test. This type of analysis helps to clarify the product's potential against the competitive nature of the category and of the retailer's strategy. In highly promoted categories, or in high-low shopping environments (versus EDLP), this measurement helps to normalize what high-low success looks like and evaluate the test item on a fair playing ground. As we have learned in past tests, where something is being sold (category and retailer) can have just as much impact on the determination of success as the product line's performance.

- **Consistency.** The *Consistency* of a product is a measure of its ability to meet certain target thresholds. Each week's sales for a test product are characterized by their percentile of sales (units or revenue) relative to the comparable products that help to define a reasonable yardstick of success. The categorization of performance against the targets identified can come at many different levels, and the better innovations have an ability to sustain specific thresholds in a consistent way over time.

The more testing we execute with our clients, the more the existence of a normative database allows us to help guide not just how an innovation performed, but also *why* any individual innovation was successful (or not). Through our extensive test modeling, we can not only interpret the relative success or failure of a new product in a test, but also understand the *reasons behind the success or failure*. This helps everyone know whether their opportunity is on track or off track, how they can make it better, and how they can prepare the innovation to be even more successful in a larger-scale launch.

AGILE, ITERATIVE, AND ENTREPRENEURIAL

A CPG company needs to carefully curate which ideas are *ready* for this level of in-store sales testing. When embedding *Burst* into an organization's stage-gate process, it's wise to refrain from using every test on every product. Not all ideas are ready for (or worthy of) an in-market test. Because it takes time and effort to produce a product, even for small-scale testing, this testing model is best for those amazing ideas that need a certain amount of real-world evidence to prove to the organization that they will be worth the effort to scale up.

At the end of the *Burst* process, sometimes the data indicates a rip-roaring success, other times the results point to something positive but with signs of caution, and sometimes the data proves the idea is a failure. All three of these testing outcomes are good learning opportunities. Proof of failure is extremely valuable because it either gives the team a chance to revamp the idea or opens up the opportunity to scrap the project before it costs the company millions of dollars.

Burst is a process that can implement real-word testing, gather real-world data, and predict a new idea's level of success in the real world. It's agile, it's iterative, and it's downright entrepreneurial. Plus, it's a clever way for a company to take risks without taking on any big risks.

A SUMMARY OF PRODUCT LAUNCH CHALLENGES AND TRANSACTIONAL TESTING

Core insights regarding the current challenges with product launches:

- Boom, Splat

- The Supermarket Jungle

- The Retailer Conundrum

- Testing Your Objectives

The spectrum of transactional testing:

1. At-Shelf Insights (ASI)

2. Weekend Tests

3. Retail Labs

4. Multichannel Retail Labs

Thus far, we've looked at the *Energize* process for incubating disruptive ideas. We've looked at the *Make* system of creative, iterative manufacturing. And now we've taken a deep dive into *Burst*, the secret to more meaningful product testing.

But these parts of the EMBR process are not the whole story. There's one more piece of the puzzle: *Roar,* a model that gives even your riskiest ideas a chance to be realized.

CHAPTER NINE

A PATH FOR THE IMPOSSIBLE: ROAR

What if you have an idea that is so disruptive, it challenges the organization just to think about it? What if there is an idea with passionate champions and proven consumer work that still feels risky to the organization? Is there a path to externalize even the ideas that seem impossible? The answer is *yes,* and that path is a process we call *Roar.*

As we've already discussed, big CPG is structured in amazing ways to launch at scale, which requires some truly impressive logistics and well-disciplined processes. *Burst* and transactional testing in a dozen stores for a few months can help validate the idea, but there are times when another step is needed. This is where the

Roar methodology comes into play. *Roar* can fill the gap and help to de-risk the proposition even more—mimicking the entrepreneurial startup process with some unique differences.

Roar starts with thinking about how to do a small-scale rollout of your product or brand for approximately one to two years in order to build confidence about its future. It gives you the opportunity to say, "We didn't just test this idea. We got it into three hundred stores, and we grew sales to this level. It has traction and the right to live. Now, the organization can feel confident about national projections and a full-scale launch." *Roar* allows a new idea to grow to a scale that makes it viable to internalize in a large company's systems.

But *Roar* is also meant to emulate the entrepreneurial journey, providing a big company with risk mitigation that goes far beyond a test. It's a way of proving out your most disruptive or risky ideas, giving them a chance to grow, change, and improve along the way. It's not simply a regional rollout of a launch, **it is a *learning journey*, an incubation process at a small scale, meant to *optimize and grow* a product or brand.** It's about giving a disruptive idea the time to live and breathe and incubate over time.

This requires an entrepreneurial process of growing:

1. Build a consumer base that drives pull versus push demand. Where big competitors prefer to spend a lot on advertising to "push" consumers into the store, entrepreneurs focus their initial activities on retailers to use their power to "pull" consumers to their brands. This can be as simple as partnering with a retail chain to do

in-store demos, or offering a retailer free cases of product in return for feature and display.

2. Build out the retail expansion more slowly and deliberately while winning at the shelf to earn the right to expand. Entrepreneurs often focus on small launches of fifty, one hundred, or three hundred stores rather than trying to go nationwide at the start. It allows them to learn, iterate, and improve upon everything it takes to make a brand grow, all while giving them time to deliver the wows that the retailer wants to see to keep the product on-shelf.

3. Continue to listen, learn, and iterate with consumers (target audience, rejectors, etc.). How are consumers using your product, and how can you improve it? Get into the points of distribution where your product is being sold and *learn* from the shopper, the store staff, and the store manager, and take that information back to the company to make your business shine.

4. Continue to listen and learn from retailer feedback. What is working in retail, and how can you drive category growth to be both a winning brand and winning manufacturer? What does the buyer want that isn't being delivered by competitors where you can pivot to and show your level of partnership?

Entrepreneurs learn all of these things as they take that journey to their first three hundred stores. So can you.

A PROCESS FOR THE RISKIEST IDEAS

What makes an idea seem very risky to a large CPG company? It could be something new to the world, something that isn't particularly intuitive and needs time to develop with consumers. Or it could be risky because it's very far from the core business without any way to slide it into the existing machinery. Whatever the case may be, leadership believes that the idea presents high risk, and it needs time to prove or grow before it can be internalized.

THE PERFECT SCENARIO

The inspiration for *Roar* occurred a decade ago when we were discussing an idea with a big client that they felt was incredibly risky. Finally, the client said to us, "What if you guys took this idea and ran with it?" We offered to externalize the risk and become the "out-of-house startup," with our client taking the role of the "angel investor." All they had to do was fund the production and our time, and we did the rest as a team of entrepreneurs.

Leading and growing ideas as a startup intuitively means leveraging an entrepreneurial approach to prove and enhance the business viability. Here is an example of how it can work:

1. Start with collaborative development or selection of an idea that is disruptive or risky enough that it requires a slow, methodical build with a high degree of learning and iteration.

2. Think about how you might be able to externalize the most challenging processes for your team and remove the barriers that are currently getting them stuck or slowing them down.

3. Reflect on who should lead the project. Consider this for a moment: is it better to hand off a project to someone who has a light plate/workload, or would you rather assign a dedicated, passionate "founder" to run the day-to-day of this operation? If you do what we do and approach the assignment of a new project as if you're picking a founder/CEO, then the framework, the leadership, and the growth model that is set up at the start may change the way you bring the innovation to life.

4. Adjust the top-down model so that your stakeholders become the investors for the startup. Set up monthly board meetings to maintain open lines of communication and oversight while the day-to-day is left to the "founder" on your team.

5. The project should consider if it needs to externally source the entire process of getting launch ready, producing at a small scale, and gaining distribution within a geography of interest. Let growth start at zero and build as quickly as sustainably possible before it gets rolled back into the larger organization.

6. Set up the project to run with a net-neutral P&L. All proceeds from the sales of the product are immediately reinvested into the brand to help drive demand and

iterate improvements. Support is done with an entrepreneurial, scrappy lens: high efficiency, grassroots, low
cost, and fast.

7. At the end of the agreed-upon time frame, identify
    whether the opportunity is going to take the path of
    (1) internalization and scale for a national launch, (2)
    growth that requires more time to gain consumer trac-
    tion, or (3) assessment that it is off track and lacking
    the legs to grow to the scale required to internalize (in
    which case, it is disbanded).

HOMEGROWN BUT EXTERNALIZED

Ideally, the end of the process, with time and ability to grow and
modify, leads to the sponsor company saying, "The rewards are
worth the required investment and resources to internalize or
scale this brand." Since this is essentially an externalized but
homegrown innovation by the investing company, it can smoothly
transition to an internal team to run with it. The big company
gets to enjoy the benefits of using an entrepreneurial system to
patiently build up and prove out an idea without burdening the
internal team to manage the incubation.

For example, imagine a CPG company has validated a new innovation that involves physically installing something into a consumer's floor. Maybe it dispenses carpet cleaner or socks for your
kids to slip into, or it's a new place for a garbage bag. Whatever

the case, it's going to require some carpentry work on the house, which will create an unusual (and bizarre) business model for the CPG company to consider.

There's no way a CPG company's leadership is going to buy into such an idea unless it has time to prove itself with real, live consumers deciding to buy, install, and live with this idea. Since this idea is so different from just putting products into jars, bags, or boxes, and since it requires very disruptive thinking, it likely can't be proved in a short period of time. The company will need more time to validate it.

An idea doesn't even have to be that far out for *Roar* to provide significant value. It could be a new product idea in a new category or placement or a temperature state outside of the company's current expertise and structure. It could be a beverage company looking to expand into food, a fast casual restaurant expanding their product to retail, or a brand that produces shelf-stable products but wants to expand into refrigerated or frozen offerings.

Every company has these kinds of tension points. When ideas or products push into those points, people start to get uncomfortable with the amount of risk that they entail—and rightly so.

"To do this, we're going to have to engineer new machinery, build a new factory, or develop new sales teams."

Suddenly, a validated, strong idea seems far too risky to pursue without some real, concrete evidence that it's going to be worth the investment. In many companies, these kinds of disruptive and risky ideas have been around for a long time. They keep popping up, being reevaluated, but the risk is always so great, no one is willing to take the next step.

"If only we could put it out there for a while and see if it gains traction. Then we'd know if it's a risk we can accept."

Roar gives you the time and patience you need to build a consumer base for these kinds of ideas. To use an example we mentioned earlier, consider the case of kombucha. It's not surprising that beverage companies ignored this unusual sour-tasting drink for so long. In many ways, it's the antithesis to what the beverage category is all about, but when smaller companies introduced it to the market, it led to a consumer revolution. In fact, the kombucha market is projected to be worth almost $8 billion by 2027.[28]

If a large CPG company had gotten on the kombucha wave early and figured out how to make it work *for themselves*, they could have ridden that wave to amazing heights. Instead, many of them jumped on the bandwagon by acquiring existing brands at a premium, after the fact.

THE MAGIC MIDDLE

Roar operates in the "magic middle," using an entrepreneurial approach while also having access to the funding, resources, and support of a big company. You get an entrepreneur with

---

28 Kunal Ahujja and Sarita Bayas, "Kombucha Market Size," Global Market Insights, June 2021, https://www.gminsights.com/industry-analysis/kombucha-market.

small-scale manufacturing capabilities who is outside of your systems and can move much faster than you ever could internally. They take your riskiest ideas and put them out there, using all of the skills of an entire cross-functional organization.

Imagine the possibilities.

THE EVOLUTION OF EMBR INTO *IGNITE*

Let's pause for just a moment. Everything we have described up to this point is applicable to individual projects, individual circumstances, and individual challenges. The EMBR process of *Energize, Make, Burst,* and *Roar* is meant to show how you can leverage an entrepreneurial approach to make your disruptive ideas happen and de-risk them for improved internal acceptance. EMBR can help you get around what is holding you back, developing new and powerful ideas, or it can simply enhance the elements you already have developed internally.

EMBR is built to help you create, iterate, classify, build, and de-risk your key business opportunities and identify in detail the consumer behavior changes they require. The next step in that process is to imagine how your innovation process can become even more impactful when you tie them all together into one larger system—a system we call *IGNITE.*

.

CHAPTER TEN

TRANSFORMATIONAL INNOVATION: *IGNITE*

Hopefully, you've been nodding your head at times throughout this book. You recognize the challenges that exist in the structures of large CPG companies and see how new strategies might solve some of them. The strategies we've presented—*Energize, Make, Burst,* and *Roar*—are designed to address roadblocks at specific points in the innovation life cycle. The *Energize* model deals with difficulties in the creation stages of an idea. The *Make* model tackles how to manufacture new ideas in a nimble way. The *Burst* model applies to problems in the product testing phase. And *Roar* gives your riskiest ideas a chance to live and breathe over an extended period of time.

What if you could approach your innovation pipeline across a platform holistically, efficiently, and iteratively in a way that weaves together the elements into one cohesive strategy? What if you innovated in a wholly different way?

Welcome to *IGNITE*.

IGNITE is partly about employing the entrepreneurial philosophy as a powerful *cycle* that crosses many different hunting grounds, platforms, concepts, and strategic opportunities, quickly iterating and testing to find the ones that can drive disruptive demand and growth. This means bringing together the *power of big* with the *best of small*.

It's also about understanding the levers you have today to pursue innovation, understanding where those levers are used and not used, and then identifying a new model.

In our endless pursuit of innovative thinking, we came across a 2017 model from Boston Consulting Group ("BCG"—a global consulting firm) that mapped out an inventory of the innovator's toolkit across a wide range of industries—from automotive, to pharmaceuticals, to energy. [29] We felt that their conceptual model worked, and with some adapting of those concepts to fit our specific CPG industry knowledge, we created and transformed those concepts into a new version that could help everyone to understand the opportunities, limitations, and gaps of the available options.

At its core, CPG companies currently have four key levers they use most often to pursue growth with innovation:

---

29   Michael Brigl et al., "Incubators, Accelerators, Venturing, and More," Boston Consulting Group, January 25, 2017, https://www.bcg.com/publications/2014/mergers-acquisitions-growth-incubators-accelerators-venturing-more.

DESCRIPTIONS

☐ **INCUBATORS/ACCELERATORS**
Supporting early stage companies on the long path past a minimal viable product (MVP)

☐ **VENTURING**
Investing in going businesses that will drive future new growth for the organization

☐ **M&A**
Acquiring capabilities & technologies that can immediately unlock new sources of revenue

☐ **INTERNAL R&D**
Efforts that increase the probability of generating technological innovation internally

INNOVATION METHODOLOGY

	INCUBATORS/ACCELERATORS
	VENTURING
	INTERNAL R&D

| M&A |

CONNECTION TO THE CORE BUSINESS

NEW

ADJACENT

CORE

1–3 YEARS → 4–7 YEARS → 7–10 YEARS

YEARS TO REALIZE REVENUE / GROWTH

- **Internal R&D:** Internal product development focuses on developing line extensions, improvements, or iterations of the company's core businesses. This model can deliver on both close-in goals and more challenging opportunities that take many years to develop.

- **Mergers & Acquisitions (M&A):** Purchasing external companies can be a great way to allow a company to gain immediate entry into a new category, a new set of benefits, or even a new geography—all with a new profit/revenue stream. Unfortunately, M&A is also the most costly way to do innovation since you have to pay a premium for purchasing the hard work that another company already developed.

- **Venturing:** This entails providing investments (smaller than M&A) that allow a company to get involved in small but growing companies and have access to their overall growth opportunity or technology. Usually, these are long-term bets that can take five to seven years to turn into fruitful results, and the risk/reward profile is small, depending on the equity stake that is taken.

- **Incubators and Accelerators:** Both of these models are meant to give CPGs access to startup ideas where high-level support, coaching, and collaboration can possibly turn very small ideas into the next category innovator. This is likely one of the longest bets, as it can easily take seven to ten years to see tangible revenue results from the opportunity.

We believe there is a gap in this model, one that can develop new high-growth spaces more easily than internal R&D, can be *less expensive* than M&A, yet can still help large CPG organizations pursue adjacent and new or disruptive innovation opportunities in a quick and more efficient model.

We propose that *IGNITE* is the path to filling in that gap and avoiding the costs of M&A:

> **IGNITE:** A new way to develop and validate disruptive ideas, and de-risk them for viable launches with the speed of entrepreneurialism and without the cost of M&A.

IGNITE does this by:

1. Being a disruptive innovation model by way of:

    a. redefining the traditional innovation roadmap,

    b. leveraging the company's unique knowledge with a skunkworks mentality and approach,

    c. building on the company's strategic focus, and

    d. de-risking and magnifying the potential for all future launches.

2. Doing more than just launching products by:

    a. driving efficiencies in the innovation journey across multiple opportunities,

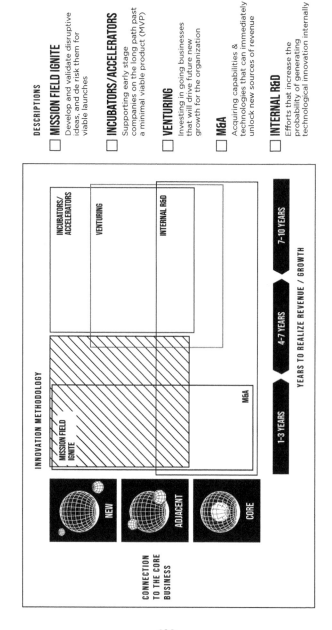

DESCRIPTIONS

☐ **MISSION FIELD IGNITE**
Develop and validate disruptive ideas, and de-risk them for viable launches

☐ **INCUBATORS/ACCELERATORS**
Supporting early stage companies on the long path past a minimal viable product (MVP)

☐ **VENTURING**
Investing in going businesses that will drive future new growth for the organization

☐ **M&A**
Acquiring capabilities & technologies that can immediately unlock new sources of revenue

☐ **INTERNAL R&D**
Efforts that increase the probability of generating technological innovation internally

    b. supporting the organization's revenue and financial targets, and

    c. giving the organization a unique right to win that competitors can't easily replicate.

3. Thinks about the growth-goal end in mind by:

    a. clarifying the vitality rate goals, and

    b. identifying the historical expectations of prior launches.

It's a radically different path forward for large CPG, one that breaks the mold of typical innovation and pipeline planning. *IGNITE* holistically innovates across many ideas quickly and nimbly to find the sparks of future growth drivers—the winning ideas to build and launch.

THE ORIGIN OF *IGNITE*

The *IGNITE* concept was born from the intersection of Jonathan's experience at OxiClean and his out-of-house Clorox disruptive innovation efforts with Carolina's work leading the Seed Group at WhiteWave Foods and launching her own tiny food startup in Boulder.

At OxiClean, Jonathan and his team established a process to go from an initial spark of an idea to on-shelf testable product in as little as six weeks. They built a model that had consumers rotating into their facility at a regular cadence, providing for an ongoing, iterative approach to building or killing ideas. As a result, they got ideas to shelf as holistically, roughly, and quickly as possible. Perfection was the enemy. Trying things out was the mission. Training their gut, and not relying on data, was the side benefit. And outputting dozens of crazy ideas into the marketplace is what happened.

If they could launch dozens of crazy ideas in a single year—perhaps only putting a single case of product in a single hardware store for a weekend—and if just one or two of those created a spark that could lead to a multimillion-dollar category-growing idea, they could win and disrupt the established brands in their category. And they did just that, growing the company from tens of millions to *a quarter of a billion* before the founders sold.

Later, while at Clorox, Jonathan continued to build out and perfect that disruptive entrepreneurial innovation model, this time with the power and resources of an industry-leading CPG supporting him. He was able to guide key internal stakeholders to see the benefits of externalizing their innovation challenges in small-scale ways and helped to build and prove out numerous product opportunities using that model. The pathway for how to make an entrepreneurial model work was tested, refined, and tested again, each time getting a little better. Jonathan was also able to see where the organization pushed back, where it got out of its comfort zone, and when it unintentionally got in its own way of making further progress.

As for Carolina, she spent nearly three years inside of a big CPG company, working on developing a model that could quickly conceptualize ideas and get them to market on a small scale. The goal was to become a demand-based category creator and win with accretive consumer targets, brands, or channels. The concept was sound, the senior leadership direction and support was best-in-class, and the right team was in place. Key internal barriers were identified, and she gained insight into the need to externalize aspects of the innovation process that created risk or caused internal angst.

On the side, Carolina was also pouring her passion into developing and launching her own paleo-friendly snack brand. Her personal nights and weekends of living the entrepreneurial life combined with her nine-to-five corporate innovation efforts were invaluable for understanding the role of the entrepreneurial model in innovation, the pathways for making it successful, and the guardrails that large organizations face when trying to be nimble.

THE OBJECTIVES OF *IGNITE*

So, what does *IGNITE* hope to accomplish?

It's easy to say, but hard to do: *IGNITE* is about changing your innovation model from a project-based linear model to a rapid, holistic, and iterative model that seeks to kick the tires on dozens of disruptive ideas in order to find the winners that will maximize growth.

It's about feeling comfortable encouraging speed, imperfection, small failures, and pivots—all while taking more chances at bat to progress multiple ideas forward and cross-pollinate to build future success.

QUOTE: *"We need a way to strategically seed and grow ideas that are constantly at risk of being killed in pursuit of fewer, bigger, better. [Sometimes the best ideas are killed] because they don't appear big enough."*

—FORTUNE 500 CPG Marketing Director of Innovation

PUTTING *IGNITE* INTO PRACTICE

By now, you're probably saying, "*IGNITE* sounds amazing, but how does it work?"

First, *IGNITE* serves CPG companies of all sizes. In large multinational companies that already have internal innovation systems in place, the *IGNITE* process creates an incubator that allows disruptive territories to be developed, tested, and de-risked close to, but just outside, the corporate engine. For midsize emerging companies that have knowledgeable marketing and R&D departments but are still developing an innovation team, *IGNITE* augments the internal capabilities and provides a blueprint for successfully building a disruptive and agile innovation arm that works on more than line extensions.

Second, we have found that there are four prerequisites for successfully running the *IGNITE* model. With these in place, a company can be ready to implement this big-visioned, fast, flexible innovation model:

- ***IGNITE* as a collaborative approach.** Theoretically, a large CPG company *could* redesign their teams to operate the *IGNITE* process internally. But as we have learned in earlier chapters, there are many hurdles to going after big bets with internally staffed disruptive innovation teams, no matter how they are organized. We believe that the most fruitful path to *IGNITE* is to form a long-term internal-external partnership. The internal team can keep everyone focused on the right strategy, application, and stakeholders while additionally managing any needed internal resources and leveraging the organization's deep knowledge base. Meanwhile, the external innovation partner can serve as the company's "skunkworks" team with the goal of more easily bringing the most disruptive ideas to life in quick and deep processes that might get constrained if run within the processes of the main organization.

- ***IGNITE* as a shift in mindsets.** The main goal of *IGNITE* is to leave behind the models you have today in order to escape the guardrails of the past. The best way to accomplish this is to align the goals and strategy of the effort to the core business objectives, and then to purposefully work around the internal challenges that are often the base reasons why things can't be done. Where the big company mentality is to pay homage to the embedded process, the entrepreneurial mentality must find a way to find a yes rather than simply listening to the reasons where the internal process says no.

- ***IGNITE* with a business approach.** The *IGNITE* model is not intended to be a purely creative endeavor but rather developed with a business approach. We have found that core, senior-level teams with deep knowledge of the client's business do better than putting creative individuals at the helm. Although innovation often feels like a creative pursuit, at some point (often quickly), it has to get real. We have heard too many stories about partners that are great at dreaming up a holistic vision of innovation, but have no idea how to execute any of it. *IGNITE* works best with experienced former CPG professionals who know how to turn strategy into ideas and ideas into reality.

- ***IGNITE* with time to iterate and adjust.** The final prerequisite for the *IGNITE* model is time. The system will achieve more if it can execute iterative product innovations on a multiyear rolling basis, with the ability to pivot and reprioritize efforts as needed at any point in the process. While this type and length of partnerships (eighteen, twenty-four, or even thirty-six months) may seem like a substantial commitment, it can be far more expeditious than the typical innovation timelines at large corporations— especially as traditional systems take a one-at-a-time process, whereas *IGNITE* is set up to develop *multiple impactful innovations over time.*

IGNITE builds a small machine within a company's big machine. It is a new way to approach innovation that leverages a company's own unique strengths. It's a faster, less costly process that can drastically lower risk for a CPG company. This model uses constant learning and rapid iteration to give ideas much greater potential for long-term success. By accelerating innovation and improving new product launches, *IGNITE* can boost a company's revenue and growth and redefines the "typical" innovation road map.

QUOTE: *"Consumers don't individually evaluate one piece at a time in the real world. Ever."*

—FORTUNE 500 CPG Director of Innovation

The keys steps included in the *IGNITE* process are:

1. The Disruptive Innovation Model

- *Redefining the traditional innovation roadmap*—In order to have something that delivers a different output than today's transitional innovation teams, we have to start with a different process that is geared to think more entrepreneurially, and one that allows more disruptive ideas to live and breathe in the system. We believe this includes the key elements of:

  ☐ Starting small and moving quickly

☐ Nurturing and growing all ideas at every stage

☐ Designing learning plans for speed and iterative insights

☐ Planning in continual refinements (R&D, packaging, concept, etc.)

☐ Avoiding looking for perfection

☐ Being decisive

☐ Demolishing current stage-gate standards and three-to-five-year innovation testing and rollouts

- *Leverage the CPG company's unique knowledge with a skunkworks mentality and approach*—Disruptive innovation always needs to connect back to the main organization to stay tuned into the strategic needs of the stakeholders, so to this end we recommend the following:

    ☐ Start with the search for real consumer-centric problems that the company can solve with steady ongoing consumer research efforts.

    ☐ Relentlessly pursue ideas with an entrepreneurial lens to identify which ones give us a right to win *and* meet the consumer's needs.

- *Build on the CPG company's strategic focus*—Use real-world learning to increase confidence and drive informed decision-making:

    ☐ Continue to test ideas in small ways before scaling and then iterate, iterate, iterate!

    ☐ Outsource what may be hard to do today or where resources are constrained.

- *De-risking and magnifying the potential for all future launches*—Take more smaller risks to find big ideas.

2. Do More Than Launch Products

- *Drive efficiencies in the innovation journey across multiple opportunities*—Innovation in large companies often stops when the new idea is handed over to the base brand, but it shouldn't be that way. Innovation needs to be an endless journey that keeps continuing, improving, and changing the core of the business to make it better. Plan on managing spot requests to fill in knowledge gaps, as needed.

- *Support the organization's revenue and financial targets*—Plan for twice as many ideas in the pipeline than needed for launches to allow for the failures and revisions that will naturally occur.

- *Give the organization a unique right to win that competitors can't easily replicate.*

3. Think About the Growth-Goal End in Mind

- *Clarify the vitality rate goals*—Leading CPG companies are using their innovation efforts as growth engines, driving upward of 10 percent of their growth from new innovations that launched in the past five years.[30] If you are a $5 billion company, and more than $500 million of last year's revenue is coming from new items (truly new innovations launched in the previous five years, not package resizes or customer customization efforts), then you are on the right path to being an innovation-driven CPG.

- *Identify the historical expectations of prior launches*— Thinking about how much growth should come from innovation also means understanding the current guardrails of your innovation launch history. If your company's biggest year-one launch happened ten years ago when product X hit $100 million, but the past nine years have seen all your other innovations launch between $10 million and $35 million, then a logical framework would be to shoot for a series "small and midsized" launches every year—that have

---

30 Martin Reeves et al., "Achieving Vitality in Turbulent Times," Boston Consulting Group, October 21, 2019, https://www.bcg.com/publications/2019/achieving-vitality-in-turbulent-times.

the power to grow big and fast over several years—to get to your goal versus banking it all on trying to find and execute that magical one or two $100 million ideas.

IGNITE is a full mind shift about your approach to innovation. It's about collaborating with or hiring a skunkworks group to outsource the things that slow you down, while honoring the internal processes that support your total efforts. That's when the magic happens.

CONCLUSION

There are so many things that big CPG companies do extremely well when it comes to innovation. They're adept at discovering consumer needs, identifying the "job to be done," and solving the real and important problems put in front of them. They can formulate, produce, and launch innovations globally in a heartbeat and with a level of perfection that is truly a modern marvel. These companies aren't doing anything wrong. The innovators at these companies aren't doing anything wrong. On the contrary, they are mostly doing everything right.

By the very nature of their size, however, big CPG companies sometimes struggle to pivot, adjust, innovate, and capture key consumer trends the way that smaller companies and nascent startups can. As a result, they sometimes lose precious opportunities to redefine and reshape the categories that they dominate.

But here's the thing: There's no need for this to happen. There's no reason this should be a trend.

A passionate entrepreneurial spirit exists within the big CPG companies. We've seen it firsthand. But innovation teams often lack the methodologies and tools necessary to accomplish their vision with the speed and agility that's requested of them. And so, just like any "job to be done" or "problem to be solved," there's an opportunity to fix what needs fixing and take the next leap forward in how innovation is pursued.

The EMBR and *IGNITE* methodologies are meant to give any big CPG company additional tools in their toolbox to pursue disruptive innovation in ways they hadn't thought possible. The innovation models we have described in this book are meant to integrate with, dovetail into, or bolt onto a company's existing systems without tearing them down.

There are lessons to be learned from the way small and nascent companies approach innovation. The EMBR philosophy shifts the innovation cycle toward an entrepreneurial methodology, creating a line of sight between ideas and successful execution. Using *Energize, Make, Burst,* and *Roar,* an innovation team can bring their most powerful opportunities to life in a small-scale, low-risk way and validate or de-risk the total opportunity for the organization so they can make forward progress. The *IGNITE* model ties together all of the parts of EMBR together into one cohesive process that leverages a company's unique strengths to get more ideas to market with greater speed.

When an innovation team's great ideas die, everyone loses out. The innovators lose out professionally and personally after championing something passionately. The company loses out on potential profits. And the consumer loses out on exciting new products brought to life by the brands they love and a company that has nothing but consumer delight and safety in mind.

We believe that by leveraging insights from our EMBR and *IGNITE* models, innovators in any CPG company have the opportunity to extend their brands to powerful and disruptive spaces. They can even build out into territories and opportunities that don't currently exist. Most importantly, they can reclaim the banner of innovation leadership from the small startups and drive the power of their categories with their assets. When this happens, the consumer wins—gaining access to new technologies and products from world-renowned brands and companies.

ONE LAST THING

We've been there. We've worked in the CPG world for decades, and we know the challenges that you—the innovation, marketing, insights, or R&D leader—constantly face. We'd love to talk to you about your innovation goals and challenges and see how we can help. We're here to support you as you drive growth and innovation within your company—partnering with you as you ideate, iterate, and succeed.

We are rooting for you,

Jonathan and Carolina

www.mission-field.com

hello@mission-field.com

(720) 242-8270

ACKNOWLEDGMENTS

JONATHAN'S ACKNOWLEDGMENTS

I owe so much to so many who have impacted me throughout my life, including my immediate family—Walter, Carmella, and Michele—who have each uniquely shaped, influenced, and molded my young self in so many special ways and who I looked up to constantly. I also want to thank my children—Aria, Ellery, and Juno—who endlessly impress me with their sense of wonder, their boundless growth, and their amazingly intuitive sense of unconstrained possibilities. And thank you, Chandi. Your infectious positivity, open heart, and brilliant mind are incredible, and I treasure and look forward to the time we have together.

I must also offer my thanks to all of my friends, whether lifelong or recent. There are too many of you to name, but I want you each to know that you've always provided me with an ongoing sense of adventure, laughter, comfort, and creativity. And of course, there's my coauthor Carolina and the entire team at Mission Field®—we have achieved so much together because of your unbridled intelligence, focused hard work, and dedication to the truth, all of which are deeply appreciated.

Lastly, I want to thank those who have made silent impacts: the mentors that I never knew I had, the guides around the corners who directed me without me ever knowing, the rocks that always had my back, and the leaders who consistently encouraged me to be my best.

To all of you, I want to say, with that much fuel in anyone's life, it's impossible not to keep "The Fire" alive and burning...so I thank you all!

CAROLINA'S ACKNOWLEDGMENTS

This amazing career, this life, and this book could not have happened without the support of many generous and wonderful people in my life. It starts with family, including the grandfathers I never knew, each of who started their own companies and laid the seeds for my entrepreneurial passions. I have vivid memories of walking my grandfather's factory floor at Vicson SA in Venezuela with a baby hard hat, full of pride and wonder at the huge machinery producing steel products (I still can't resist a plant tour).

Also, my parents, who provided a rich and interesting childhood full of travel, open possibilities, and a sense that I could do anything with hard work and perseverance. And to my older brother, who has a brilliant success story of his own and is my biggest champion and confidant—thank you for talking shop and challenging my thinking to make me better and sharper. Most importantly, to my son, Duncan, who is the most persistent and impressive young man I know—I can't wait to see where your passion takes you.

I've had the privilege of so many strong mentors along the way, the first of which was Kristina Jetton way back in the Mandarin Oriental hotel days. Kristina, I can't thank you enough for those early opportunities, for believing in me, and for becoming a lifelong friend. Thank you to Susan Felz, Germaine, Susan LS, Tiffany, Trevor, Molly, Jason, Carlos, Alan, and so many others who shaped my real-world education over the years.

I fancied myself a CPG marketer through and through until Jonathan gave me a call. I'm glad I have had the opportunity to ride this rocket ship with you and build out Mission Field®. You are the best business partner I could have asked for. Caragh, Julie, Julia, and Stacey—you rock. I am grateful beyond words.

ABOUT THE AUTHORS

Jonathan Tofel is the founder and CEO of Mission Field®. Before helping companies like PepsiCo, General Mills, and Kellogg's create disruptive innovations, Jonathan worked in Brand Management at P&G, Marketing and Innovation at OxiClean, and was an entrepreneurial consultant for The Clorox Company. Jonathan has founded two consultancies and continues to design and implement models for rapid innovation.

Carolina Sasson is the Chief Operating Officer at Mission Field®, where she embraces a holistic, iterative approach to help Fortune 500 clients develop big ideas. Starting her marketing career at P&G, Carolina launched a natural food startup in Boulder, Colorado, before spending a decade at Whitewave Foods and eventually leading The Seed Group, an internal innovation incubator.